The Last Days of

INDUSTRIAL STEAM

– ERIC SAWFORD –

The driver of *George B*, Hunslet 680 of 1898, pulls a length of chain towards the loaded wagons prior to moving them to the finishing shed on the Dinorwic Slate Quarries Co. Ltd line at Llanberis. All around waste slate litters the sides of the track. Two locomotives were usually to be found working on the lower level, with others on the higher levels.

THE LAST DAYS OF
INDUSTRIAL STEAM

– ERIC SAWFORD –

ALAN SUTTON

First published in the United Kingdom in 1991 by
Alan Sutton Publishing Ltd · Phoenix Mill · Stroud · Gloucestershire

First published in the United States of America in 1992 by
Alan Sutton Publishing Inc. · Wolfeboro Falls · NH 03896–0848

Reprinted in 1995

British Library Cataloguing in Publication Data

Sawford, Eric
The last days of industrial steam.
I. Title
385.54

ISBN 0–86299–915–4

Library in Congress Cataloging in Publication Data applied for

Typeset in 9/10 Palatino.
Typesetting and origination by
Alan Sutton Publishing Limited.
Printed and bound in Great Britain by
WBC, Bridgend, Mid Glam.

Introduction

The working industrial steam locomotive has become part of our railway heritage. With the march of time diesels replaced many of the steam engines, while closures of manufacturing companies, collieries, steelworks, etc. consigned many locomotives to the cutter's torch. Fortunately, much of this coincided with the beginnings of the railway preservation movement. Many redundant steam (and diesel) locomotives were snapped up, often for little more than scrap value. These veteran engines, now resplendent with shining brass and paintwork, can be seen at various preservation centres throughout the country. The final section of this book shows how some of these now look in preservation.

Within the pages of this book are a selection of my own photographs taken during the 1950s and '60s, many showing systems which are now but memories, nothing remaining on site to indicate that an industrial concern had once been there, let alone a busy railway system. Where once massive steelworks with extensive sidings operated throughout the day and night, lighting up the sky, large housing and industrial estates can now be found. Readers who remember the industrials during the period, will doubtless have vivid memories of them, while the enthusiasts who cannot recall working industrial steam, will be enthralled by the wide variety of motive power to be found in those seemingly distant days, especially the 1950s when many real gems were still gallantly carrying out their duties, as they had for a great many years before.

Standard gauge rail systems operating their own locomotives were sometimes extensive with a large fleet of locomotives and many miles of their own track. Included in these were the large industrial complexes of docks and harbours, not forgetting the numerous mineral systems which threaded their way through the countryside. Ironstone and coal between them accounted for a great many of the industrial locomotives' activities. On the other hand many locations had just one or two locomotives, often kept in immaculate condition and carefully maintained by the driver. Most of the larger gasworks and electricity generating stations also had their own locomotives, normally used daily to handle incoming fuel supplies.

In the mountains of North Wales the sight and sounds could originate from a narrow gauge engine, shunting slate wagons high up on one of the slate quarry galleries. During the heyday of the Welsh slate industry many quarries existed around the Llanberis and Bethesda areas, each with their small narrow gauge locomotives. Among these were veteran De Winton vertical boiler locomotives built at nearby Caernarvon. Little remains of these slate quarry systems, apart from mountainous waste slate tips which will be with us for a great many years to come.

Many narrow gauge lines also existed elsewhere, together with other non-standard gauge systems of metre and even 4 ft gauge. One 4 ft gauge line was the Padarn Railway which handled slate from the Dinorwic quarries at Llanberis, to the railhead on the North Wales coast. Many of the locomotives which worked on the quarry systems are preserved. For many years the Dinorwic slate quarries kept the veteran *Fire Queen* in a shed at Llanberis. This 0–4–0 tender engine was built by Northfleet Ironworks in 1848 and supplied new to the line, with sister engine *Jenny Lind*, which was scrapped way back in 1886. This interesting engine can now be seen at Penrhyn Castle museum, not far away from where it once worked, having now been in preservation for over 100 years!

While many treasures of the locomotive world had been withdrawn in the years prior to those covered by this book, those still in service were fascinating. Many veterans were still at work, some dating back to the 1870s, with odd instances of even earlier survivals. One could also often find locomotives which had long since been withdrawn – dumped and out of use, many still intact apart from the ravages of time, metal dealers and exposure to the elements; others having been cannibalized to keep another veteran in service. At some locations up to ten, or even more, withdrawn engines were to be found quietly rusting away, examples of such derelicts are to be seen within the photographs contained in this book. Many of the locomotives once thought beyond repair in those days have been restored with the aid of modern technology, restored and now work again.

In larger concerns operating a fleet of locomotives, shed duties and locomotive maintenance were carried out by staff employed for the purpose. At the small systems 'run on a shoestring', drivers were responsible for just about everything on their locomotives. This ranged from fire-lighting, maintenance, coaling and cleaning, which in a lot of cases was low in the list of priorities, to actually driving the locomotive. However, some of these one-man-band operations resulted in an immaculate locomotive, which ran beautifully, the driver concerned taking a great pride in 'his' engine.

Visits to these industrial systems were fairly easy to arrange. For instance, I recall in 1955, after having written and obtained permission to visit and photograph the locomotives of the Kettering Iron & Coal Co. Ltd, it was with a certain amount of disappointment, that I arrived at the narrow gauge shed, on what turned out to be a very wet gloomy mid-November day. However, the staff soon made me welcome, and I was free to observe the workings of the 3 ft gauge quarry locomotives, with plenty to keep them occupied. The neat Manning Wardle 0–6–0 saddle tanks were working trains of wooden-bodied wagons, fitted with wooden buffers, to and from the quarries. The lightly laid track was typical of many industrial locations with numerous kinks, bumps and dips, as it threaded its way through the countryside to the quarry.

The locomotives were housed in a fairly modern brick-built shed, where maintenance work was also carried out. The engines were all well maintained and reasonably clean. Coaling was performed by hand, the coal being stacked on the footplate. All the locomotives carried a sizeable toolbox, and the crew were expected to deal with any problems that arose which were within their capabilities, including re-railing locomotives and wagons if necessary!

In the yard stood a veteran Black Hawthorn 0–4–0 saddle tank. On such a wet day, one could not help but notice the virtually non-existent protection for the crew. It consisted of just a weatherboard with two round windows, without glass, and even when working forward it could offer little protection – certainly none when working bunker first. An enjoyable day could easily be spent at such a location, no one would hurry you, in fact employees took little notice, except to pass the time of day, and perhaps enquire why you had chosen to photograph their railway system, and often what seemed to them, long obsolete motive power.

The day's activities on an individual line were unpredictable. I well recall on a visit to Irchester watching and photographing a tank engine running light; the next moment there was a loud bang and the engine became derailed – completely blocking the running line to the quarry. Until the offending engine was re-railed nothing could move. In true industrial fashion jacks and large pieces of timber soon appeared, and after a short time the engine was restored to the track and driven off, and life returned to normal on the railway, the scene was recorded on film and is included in this book.

The larger standard gauge systems showed a totally different face, operating very much along conventional railway guidelines. Systems such as those which existed at Stewart & Lloyds Steelworks, Corby, operated a large locomotive fleet. Here was a very well equipped depot, which provided back-up services to the varied locomotive designs which operated there around the clock. Many engines were at work at all times, providing a flow of incoming materials, often shunting wagons containing finished products, ready for despatch to customers over a wide area. Two or three other locomotives were responsible for removing waste products from the works and conveying them to the slag tips.

Industrial locomotives were often worked hard, as the loads which they were called upon to handle were considerable, not only in locations such as steelworks and heavy industry, but also at quarries where to get the ore from the quarry would often involve a stiff climb out. The sight of an industrial engine being worked flat out, on very greasy rails, certainly provided a spectacular sight often requiring a charge at any incline.

By far the most common type of industrial locomotive was the saddle tank of 0–4–0 or 0–6–0 construction. This was followed by side tanks of many designs from a wide range of locomotive builders. Crane tanks, Garratts and engines such as *Monarch*, the 0–4–4–0T Bagnall on the Bowaters system at Sittingbourne, Kent, added variety. Ex-mainline locomotives were also to be found in industrial service. Ex-Great Western Railway locomotives from the Welsh valleys travelled far and wide, several examples once owned by the Cardiff, Taff Vale and Barry railways were to be found in the possession of the National Coal Board in the North East. In later years the Coal Board purchased more up-to-date GWR designs as they were withdrawn from BR service. Three 15XX class Panniers found their way to Warwickshire, and other Panniers of 16XX and 94XX and several 57XX class also worked for several years at various South Wales collieries.

Surprisingly, not very many ex-Southern Railway locomotives found their way into industrial service, two SECR P class 0–6–0 tanks, nos 31178 and 31556 were to survive into industrial service and on into preservation, together with a LBSCR E1 class and LSWR B4 dock tank. Locomotives originating from railways which were later to become part of the LMS which were sold for industrial use, included several North Staffs Railway tanks. These were owned by the NCB at Manchester, together with two examples each of locomotives from the Lancashire & Yorkshire and the Furness Railway. The LNER group was represented by 0–6–0 'Austerity' saddle tanks and two ex-North Eastern locomotives. A veteran Great Eastern survivor was to be found at Fairfields shipyard, now this locomotive is on display at North Woolwich station museum.

Standard gauge designs by Andrew Barclay of Kilmarnock and Pecketts of Bristol were very common, and found throughout the country, while six other major builders were well represented, Avonside, Hunslet, Hudswell Clarke and Hawthorn Leslie, together with Bagnalls and Robert Stephenson, various other locomotive builders had many engines still going strong, while a few were down to sole survivors.Not all the industrial locomotives of the period had been built by British companies; examples of designs by French and German companies were to be found, mostly on the narrow gauge systems.

Looking back during production of this book, it became apparent to me that the 1950s were the ideal years to visit the industrial locations, when a letter requesting a visit addressed to the Works Manager or Chief Engineer, would usually result in permission being granted. However, as the 1960s approached many of the real veterans had been cut up or dismantled, and while the end of steam on British Railways was rapidly approaching, many more enthusiasts turned their attention to the industrials. Unfortunately, some of the enthusiasts' activities resulted in visitors not being so welcome at remaining locations. Now the wheel has turned full circle, many lines are but memories, while those that survive, have diesel locomotives, which interest only the dedicated enthusiast.

Often in the railway press, reference is made to the quality of photographic equipment available years ago, compared with that of today . Most of the photographs were taken with a trusty Agfa 'Isolette' camera, producing $2\frac{1}{4}$ in square negatives. This reliable camera travelled a great many miles, on both industrial and BR visits. In the 1950s the types of film available were limited, for many years Ilford FP3 was used. I, like so many other railway photographers, started using colour materials in the mid-1960s. Armed with today's array of photographic equipment, i.e. SLR cameras, telephoto lens, zooms etc., many more interesting and varied shots would have been possible, especially at different locations – now the hardware exists – the working subjects have gone!

Unlike their mainline counterparts, where mostly only the top line passenger locomotives carried names, the naming of industrial locomotives was commonplace, just about every possible name was to be found – ranging from Christian names, to place and location names, while some carried names with a local connection. Often visitors were left wondering what a particular locomotive was named after, especially when the engine had been transferred to the location from a previous home a great many miles away.

During the 1960s many systems were no longer economical, quarry lines closed, blast furnaces were dismantled, and the companies still having a railway system turned over to the diesel locomotive. At this time, a few enthusiast specials were operated, some using vans (where they existed), such as the Stewart & Lloyds minerals system, while others used their rolling stock and open wagons, normally carrying iron ore or other minerals. The sight of a train loaded with enthusiasts in open wagons crossing a public highway, such as the 'enthusiasts' day' at S&L Minerals, Wellingborough, must certainly have raised the eyebrows of a few passing motorists.

Many of the photographs will be of great interest to modellers, especially those of the narrow gauge lines, for modellers with limited space, a neat little layout can be constructed, based on a quarry railway, and its wide variety of locomotives. Others may be interested in a particular design or an individual locomotive, while to some this typical industrial background will prove of interest. With the growth of the preservation movement, many of the remaining industrial locomotives were to become very attractive propositions, often they could be obtained at knock down prices, or even at scrap price. Many of these are today working hard on various lines throughout the country, those that were once work-stained now haul passenger services in immaculate condition, shining like new pins, with gleaming paintwork and brasswork, carefully looked after by dedicated steam enthusiasts.

Narrow gauge locomotives were much sought after. The Hunslet Engine Company has many fine examples in preservation, for instance thirty-nine examples of 0–4–0ST are still with us today, originating from three Welsh quarry systems: the Dinorwic,

Penrhyn and the Pen-y-Orsedd. Of the total, all except six are in various parts of this country, many superbly restored and hard at work on preservation lines.

Many other engine builders are represented by surviving narrow gauge locomotives some being more widely known than others, for instance, the four Peckett tanks of Rugby Portland Cement Company, examples of which are illustrated in this book. *Jurassic*, *Triassic* and *Mesozoic* are preserved in this country, the fourth engine of the group, *Liassic*, was another locomotive to be preserved in Canada.

Often when looking back at the derelict locomotives found at some of the locations – smokeboxes rotted through, tanks, cabs etc. rusted away to paper-thinness, to say nothing of the condition of the boilers, fireboxes and missing running gear, it is indeed a great credit to the engineering abilities of the preservation movement, that the many locomotives, judged by some to be long past repair and restoration, can now be found in excellent mechanical condition, restored to almost their original state when new, some having had new parts specially made for them.

After the Second World War a great many ex-WD 'Austerity' 0–6–0 saddle tanks built at this time became available. A considerable number were purchased by the National Coal Board, being distributed to many collieries throughout the country, here again, many eventually finding their way into preservation, and being joined by locomotives constructed after the war to the same design, while further examples were purchased direct from Ministry of Defence establishments. These powerful locomotives have provided invaluable motive power to numerous steam centres, where they often handle some of the heaviest loads.

Of the great many industrials preserved, it would be impossible to go into detail on all. However, we are fortunate that we have a wide selection with us today, some being sole survivors from little known engine builders, some dating back over a hundred years, of which the Haydock Foundry 0–6–0 WT *Bellerophon* built around 1874 now once again in working order on the Keighley and Worth Valley railway, is a good example. Naturally, with the large numbers of Andrew Barclays, Hudswell Clarkes, Pecketts and later Robert Stephenson and Hawthorn designs which became available, a great many have survived. Of these, those of Andrew Barclay far outnumber any other builder, with approximately a hundred standard gauge survivors of the locomotives constructed by this popular Scottish company.

As readers progress through this book, the wide variety of industrial locomotives in industrial steam's last few years will become readily apparent. Many are now regretfully no longer with us, no doubt some of those would have made excellent preservation subjects. We are, however, extremely fortunate that those which survive well illustrate British engineering, and are an important part of our railway heritage.

The Narrow Gauges

Here are some of the narrow gauge systems still to be found in the 1950s and '60s, when some of these extremely interesting rail operations had already ceased working. Those that did remain operational were certainly of great interest, narrow gauge engines having a fascination of their own.

At Sittingbourne Kent, the extensive rail systems of the Bowaters United Kingdom, Pulp and Paper Mills Ltd were extremely active, worked by an interesting selection of motive power. The rail system throughout the works area was 2 ft 6 in gauge. Most of the locomotives had been supplied new to the railway over the years, one notable exception was *Chevallier*, a Manning Wardle, which came to the line from the Chattenden & Upnor railway in 1950. Three neat little Kerr Stuart 0–4–2 saddle tanks built 1905–8, carrying the names *Premier*, *Leader*, and *Excelsior*, and a fourth *Melior*, built in 1924, were in the company's locomotive fleet, together with Kerr Stuart 0–6–2 T *Superior* built in 1920. The other seven locomotives were Bagnalls, two of which were fireless locomotives. Another locomotive built by the same company was the unusual *Monarch*, an 0–4–4–0T built as recently as 1953, and later to find its way to the Welshpool & Llanfair Railway. The remaining Bagnalls were 0–6–2 tanks named *Conqueror*, *Alpha*, *Triumph* and *Superb*, of which *Conqueror* was the oldest, being built in 1922. The last to be supplied was *Superb* in 1940, all were sturdy and powerful workhorses. The five Kerr Stuarts survive, three still at the site where part of the railway is operated by a preservation group, The Sittingbourne & Kemsley Railway. Of the Bagnall 0–6–2 tanks and the Bagnall fireless *Unique*, three are still at Sittingbourne. The sole Manning Wardle, built in 1915 and named *Chevallier* is preserved on the Whipsnade Railway.

In the same county, British Insulated Callender Cables Belvedere operated two 3 ft 6½ in gauge Bagnalls, works nos 2133–4, built in 1924. Both these engines *Woto* and *Sir Tom* are in preservation. In Surrey two veteran Fletcher Jennings 0–4–0 tanks, built in 1880, survived on the 3 ft 2 in gauge line of the Dorking Greystone Lime Company at Bletchworth. These engines, named *Townsend Hook* and *William Findlay*, were both supplied new to the line. Fortunately these two historic locomotives are still with us, one in the same county in which it worked for many years.

Northamptonshire was of considerable interest during the period. At Cranford, the neat little Bagnall 2 ft gauge saddle tank *Pixie*, built in 1919 was still working, this engine was later to move to neighbouring Leicestershire on the well known Cadeby Light Railway. Not many miles away from Cranford, three powerful metre gauge Pecketts of a modern design were hard at work at Stewart & Lloyds Minerals' Wellingborough ironstone quarries. It was a line very much in the public eye, as it crossed the busy

Finedon to Wellingborough road on a level crossing. Of the three locomotives, smart in their dark green S&L livery, which worked the line until eventual closure, two had been supplied new in 1934, Peckett works nos 1870–1, the third joining them in 1942. All three survive, and are at present preserved. By far the most interesting narrow gauge line in the county of Northamptonshire was to be found at Kettering, here again were ironstone quarries, but veteran locomotives were employed. The company was the Kettering Iron & Coal Co. Ltd., which was to become a subsidiary of the large Stewart & Lloyds operation, only three years before the furnaces which were on the site, closed in 1959. The quarry system was a 3 ft gauge line, operated by two Black Hawthorn 0–4–0 saddle tanks, which offered precious little in the way of cab protection for the crew, having been built way back in 1879 and 1885. In addition there was a Sentinel of 1926 vintage, but pride of place must go to the three sturdy Manning Wardle 0–6–0 saddle tanks, all supplied new to the line, two before the end of the century, and the third not long after, in 1906. These engines were of a neat design, having a cab which certainly offered more protection than the spartan conditions of the Black Hawthorns. On all the locomotives long brass nameplates were carried, reading 'Kettering Furnaces', followed by their number. All the engines were well maintained mechanically, and kept in reasonably clean condition. Although it is now many years since the line closed, two of its engines still survive, one each of the Black Hawthorns and Manning Wardles.

Moving across the country, another worthwhile visit was to the Rugby Portland Cement Co. Ltd works at Southam in Warwickshire. Four neat little 0–6–0 Peckett saddle tanks worked the quarry system, which was laid to a gauge of 1 ft 11½ in. All the engines varied in detail. One of the four survivors still active in the 1950s was the first of six Pecketts. Two were scrapped in 1943, together with the only other steam locomotive, a 1924-built Bagnall 0–4–0ST. The oldest Peckett *Jurassic* arrived in 1903 with others following in 1906, 1909, 1911, 1913 and 1923, the last three engines supplied were in the final four to work the line, *Liassic*, *Triassic* and *Mesozoic*. All the Pecketts survive, three in various parts of this country, the fourth is now a long way from its sisters, in Canada.

North Wales provided the largest number of working and surviving narrow gauge locomotives of the period. Here in daily use were many veterans, some working high in the mountains on exposed slate quarry galleries. The Welsh slate quarries having operated steam locomotives for a great many years, all now long gone, as has a large proportion of the slate industry. On the coast at Penmaenmawr veteran 3 ft gauge *Watkin* stood derelict, a De Winton vertical boiler locomotive built in 1893 at nearby Caernarvon. This unusual engine was owned by Penmaenmawr & Welsh Granite Co. Ltd. Several De Wintons survived in the 1950s, surprisingly, including a veteran of 1878 *Penmaen* and *Llanfair* built in 1895, other locomotives of the same type on this site having been scrapped years before. When one looks at the photographs of *Watkin*, the ravages of exposure to salt-laden air can clearly be seen. However, such is the interest in preservation of our railway history, that these three interesting and unusual locomotives can still be seen today.

Inland at Bethesda, the Penrhyn Quarries Ltd operated. These were formerly Lord Penrhyn's slate quarries until 1952. At one time these were the largest slate workings in the world, operating an extensive rail system both in the quarries and at the Penrhyn Railway, used for transporting slate to Port Penrhyn, near Bangor. On arrival at Port Penrhyn, the slate was transhipped to sea or rail. After a great many years of service the Port Penrhyn line closed in 1962, being lifted and the track sold three years later. During its long life, the Penrhyn Railway had been operated by horses and gravity, until steam took over, even operating its own passenger service for quarry men and company employees until 1951.

Like so many of the Welsh narrow gauge lines, De Wintons from nearby Caernarvon, were the Penrhyn's first steam locomotives, two of which still survive today , both being built over one hundred years ago. Seventeen Hunslets were employed on various sections, together with a selection of other locomotive builders' designs which had mostly been purchased from other narrow gauge lines, these included Bagnalls, Andrew Barclays, Kerr Stuarts and Avonsides. A solitary Orenstein & Koppel called *Eigiau* built in Berlin, also came to the Penrhyn in 1929 from the Aluminium Corporation Ltd. Another sole survivor was *Bronllwyd*, a Hudswell Clarke 0–4–0 WT of 1930, purchased from Surrey County Council in 1934. Having visited the line on two occasions, I can well recall the row of very rusty derelicts standing near the workshops, some having been out of use for years, joined from time to time by another of the locomotives. Careful study of this line up reveals the amount of work involved in restoration, when one sees a locomotive, once a part of this sad scene, today. The high standard of work carried out, makes it difficult to recognize it as once being derelict.

Engines from Penrhyn have travelled far and wide. By far the most widely known are the Hunslets *Linda* and *Blanche*, which before and after rebuilding as 2–4–0 saddle tanks, have proved mainstays of the Ffestiniog Railway.

In the Nantille Valley, the Pen-Yr-Orsedd slate quarries operated a fleet of 2 ft gauge steam locomotives, among them the locally well-known De Wintons. A Pen-Yr-Orsedd locomotive had the honour of being the very last De Winton to steam in industrial service. The line's other steam motive power was provided by three Hunslets, *Britomart*, *Sybil* and *Una*, and a 1917 0–4–0 tank, *Diana*, built by Kerr Stuart. *Britomart* is now occasionally seen in steam on the Ffestiniog Railway.

The other major slate concern active during the 1950s and '60s was the Dinorwic Slate Quarries Co. Ltd at Llanberis, overlooking Mount Snowdon. At this location both a 1 ft $10\frac{3}{4}$ in gauge system and the Padarn Railway, a 4 ft line linking Llanberis with the coast for transhipment of slate, existed. On the Padarn, steam had reigned supreme since the two 0–4–0 locomotives were supplied in 1848, one of which, *Fire Queen*, has been preserved for well over one hundred years, her sister *Jenny Lind* was not so lucky, being scrapped about 1886 when *Fire Queen* was withdrawn and laid aside for preservation by this far sighted company. The engine spent many years in a stone building, opened occasionally for visitors. The locomotives which replaced the veterans were three Hunslet 0–6–0 tanks, one being built in 1882, the others in 1886 and 1895. All were named, being known as *Dinorwic*, *Amalthaea* (originally *Pandora*) and *Velinheli*. When the line closed two of the locomotives were still intact, although one had been dismantled on site. All three were, however, scrapped at the same time in 1963.

Motive power for the 1 ft $10\frac{3}{4}$ in system came mainly from Hunslets, the exceptions being a Bagnall, an Avonside and an Andrew Barclay design. Locomotives built by other companies and used on the Dinorwic had long since disappeared. Considerable changing of locomotive names took place during the line's history. It fell to a Dinorwic Hunslet, *Holy War*, to be the last locomotive to work regularly in a Welsh quarry, completing many years of industrial service in 1967. On most days at least two locomotives could be found working on the bottom level of the quarry. Seeing a Dinorwic locomotive for the first time, one could not help but be impressed by its outward appearance and its mechanical condition which always seemed to be good. Twenty-three different Hunslets worked on the Dinorwic quarry lines, luckily most have been preserved.

Many other narrow gauge locomotives were still in existence in the country in the 1950s, some still working, while others had lain disused for considerable periods. The photographs chosen illustrate some of the wide variety of non-standard gauge locomotives operative.

This view shows *Liassic* at the head of a typical train. As can be seen, the footplate conditions were very cramped indeed. Rugby Portland Cement Company had four of these Pecketts during the mid-1950s, all varying in detail. This one is P1216/09, two other similar engines had worked on the system, both being scrapped in 1943.

Rugby Portland Cement Co. locomotive shed at Southam, with *Triassic* raising steam at the start of the day. *Triassic* was built by Pecketts in 1911 as works no. 1270. This particular engine was rebuilt at Southam in 1951, and like her other three sisters is now in preservation. At this time *Mesozoic* was out of service and under repair in the shed.

The Peckett, *Jurassic*, is seen here passing the locomotive depot with a train consisting of four loaded wagons. Time was running out for the rail system at the time this photograph was taken in 1954, in just two years the tramway was to be superseded by road transport. *Jurassic* was built in 1903 and was the oldest of the locomotives on the system.

Jurassic heads a train of narrow gauge wagons on the 1 ft 11½ in gauge rail system of the Rugby Portland Cement company at Southam, Warwickshire, on a bright November day in 1954. The engine is a Peckett, no. 1008, built in 1903 and supplied new. It was the oldest of the four locomotives surviving here at that time.

This interesting photograph shows the cab layout of *Dolbadarn*. Note the wagon used as a tender, also the chains and coal on the footplate itself. *Dolbadarn* was a member of the Dinorwic 'Port' class, all members of this small class were originally built with cabs.

Dolbadarn runs slowly round the quarry line to pick up its next load. In the right-hand side of the picture some of the slate dressing sheds can be seen. *Dolbadarn* was built by the Hunslet Engine Co. in 1922 as works no. 1430, this engine is preserved at the Llanberis Lake Railway.

This photograph is typical of the locations in which the slate quarry locomotives worked. Here *George B* slowly moves its train of loaded slate wagons on their way to the dressing sheds. Note the background showing where slate has been quarried in the past.

George B stands during a break in duties at the Dinorwic Quarries, Llanberis. The driver kept this locomotive in excellent condition. *George B* was built by Hunslet's in Leeds in 1898 and was supplied new to the company. It is works no. 680 and is now privately owned. Note the solid buffers.

The Dinorwic Slate Quarry system at Llanberis was 1 ft 10¾ in gauge. On 16 July 1964 *Dolbadarn* was busily shunting on the main level. Several Hunslets were operated by the company, *Dolbadarn* was no. 1430 of 1922. The locomotive is still in North Wales working not far away on the Llanberis Lake Railway.

Most of the Dinorwic Slate Quarries Co. Ltd's locomotive stock was built by the Hunslet Engine Co. Ltd. In June 1963 *Cackler* was stored in the workshops, it is now preserved in Norfolk, and is in regular use at Thursford Steam Museum.

This interesting Bagnall 0–4–0ST *Pixie* will be very well known to visitors to the Cadeby Light Railway. In this photograph *Pixie* is seen in its wooden locomotive shed at Cranford, Northamptonshire, where it was used by Stavely Minerals on the ganistering tramway. *Pixie* is works no. 2090 built in 1919, having been transferred to Cranford, from Pitsford in the same county in 1949. Here it was photographed in December 1955.

One of the Penrhyn locomotives which was to make a long journey to the United States was *Marchlyn*, photographed shunting on 12 June 1963. This neat little Avonside, no. 2067, was built in 1933, moving to the Penrhyn system in 1936 with its sister locomotive no. 2066, both coming from Durham County Water Board at Wearhead.

Nesta, Hunslet 704 of 1899, was a member of the Penrhyn 'Small Quarry' class and is seen here with loaded wagons. In the background a steam-powered excavator can be seen. The bleakness of the situations that the Penrhyn and other quarry locomotives worked in is clearly illustrated by the background.

Two Avonside Engine Company 0–4–0Ts were among the locomotives at Penrhyn, both being purchased from the Durham County Water Board in 1936. The picture shows *Ogwen*, AE2066, of 1933, on duty on one of the upper levels on a wet and dismal June day in 1962. Both the Avonsides were sold to the USA in 1966.

An interesting photograph of the Andrew Barclay 0–4–0WT, *Gegin*, showing the improvised tender, and in the misty background one of the slate dressing sheds at the Penrhyn can be seen. Note where the oil can is carried, immediately behind the front buffer beam.

Winifred was another of the Hunslets owned by the Penrhyn quarries. The locomotive is seen here shunting on one of the lower levels. *Winifred* was a member of the Penrhyn 'Port' class, none of which were built with cabs, the design incorporating a dropped rear footplate. *Winifred*, Hunslet no. 364 of 1885, is now in the United States. Note the interesting intersection of the points in the foreground.

Years of exposure to the elements had certainly taken their toll on *Stanhope*, Kerr Stuart no. 2395 of 1917, standing among other derelict locomotives in the Penrhyn slate quarry yard at Bethesda, North Wales. The slate quarries at Penrhyn were the largest in the world in their heyday, having an extensive fleet of locomotives originating from several different builders.

Although several of the derelict locomotives at Penrhyn looked in a completely hopeless condition, surprisingly most survived. This one is an Orenstein & Koppel of Berlin, Germany, 0–4–0WT, works no. 5668, built in 1912. The locomotive was owned by the Aluminium Corporation, moving to Penrhyn in 1929. This photograph of *Eigiau* was taken on 25 June 1962, within less than a year the locomotive was moved for preservation.

The rusty remains of one of the De Winton vertical boiler locomotives, built in 1877, on the Penrhyn scrap road. Several of the Welsh slate quarries operated De Wintons, built not far away at Caernarvon. Several derelict locomotives stood in the Penrhyn scrap road in 1962, most have been purchased for preservation.

The sad remains of *Bronllwyd* lying in a derelict row at Penrhyn, this 0–6–0WT was built by Hudswell Clarke in 1930 as works no. 1643. The locomotive had been stripped of boiler and cab to rebuild *Pamela* in 1951.Even these remaining parts have survived into preservation.

Gegin an Andrew Barclay 0–4–0WT, was built in 1931 as works no. 1991. Two years previous to its fellow, *Glyder*, it came to Penrhyn from the Durham County Water Board at Wearhead in 1936. The engine is photographed in typical slate quarry lower level surroundings, note the slate tip in the background and pieces strewn around. This engine also travelled to the USA to be preserved in Tennessee.

High up on one of the bleak upper levels of the Penrhyn slate quarries *Nesta* heads a train of typical slate wagons. In the background can be seen one of the slate quarries cut into the mountainside. *Nesta* was sold for preservation in the United States.

Glyder was the other Andrew Barclay on the Penrhyn purchased by the Penrhyn quarries from the Durham County Water Board in 1938. When photographed in 1962 it was in excellent condition, although the lower cabside shows marks from encounters with slate. In the background one of the inclines used can be seen. This engine was shipped to the USA in 1966.

Blanche seen here receiving attention in the Penrhyn workshops on 12 June 1963, surrounded by interesting equipment used in the maintenance of the Penrhyn fleet of locomotives. *Blanche* was built as an 0–4–0ST by Hunslet's of Leeds in 1893 as works no. 589. This locomotive and sister engine *Linda* 590/1893 were supplied new to the line. Both have been on the Ffestiniog railway for a number of years, performing much excellent service, having in recent years been converted to 2–4–0s, and running with a tender attached.

Jubilee 1897 stands forlornly in the scrap-yard at Penrhyn slate quarries on 25 June 1962. This interesting narrow gauge Manning Wardle was built in 1897 as works no. 1382. Fortunately, this engine has been preserved at the Tywyn Narrow Gauge Museum, moving there a few months after this photograph was taken.

31

Lilla was different from many of the Hunslet 0–4–0STs on the Penrhyn in that it has a domed boiler, straight running-plate and cab. Here the Hunslet, works no. 554, built in 1891, stands in the derelict row, looking remarkably intact apart from coupling rods. This locomotive is now preserved at the Kew Bridge Engine Museum.

Judging by the external condition of *Lilian* a few years had passed since the locomotive was last in steam. This engine is a member of the Penrhyn 'Port' class, built by Hunslet's in 1883 as works no. 317. The members of this class were not fitted with cabs and had a distinctive dropped rear footplate. Fortunately, *Lilian* has been preserved and is now at the Launceston Steam Railway.

Two locomotives built by Kerr Stuart & Co. Ltd were in the locomotive fleet of the Penrhyn, both were derelict during the early 1960s, this one is *Sgt Murphy*, an 0–6–0T built in 1918 as works no. 3117. All name and works plates had been removed from the derelict engine.

Andrew Barclay no. 1954 was under repair at Granton gasworks on 22 August 1955. Scenes such as this were very familiar on industrial systems, as often facilities did not exist for repair of locomotives under cover, especially if it involved lifting the engine completely.

Triumph was built by Bagnalls in 1934 as works no. 2511. Two systems were in use at Bowaters United Kingdom Paper Mills Ltd where *Triumph* worked; the standard at Ridham Dock and the 2 ft 6 in gauge system used elsewhere.

10.7.67

This Kerr Stuart 0–4–2ST *Excelsior* was lying out of use when photographed, and judging by appearances it had not steamed for some considerable time.

10.7.67

At first glance this photograph gives the impression of a locomotive in the Cuban sugar plantations. The scene is of *Alpha* heading a train on the Bowaters system. *Alpha* is an 0–6–2T, built by Bagnall as works no. 2472 in 1932. Note the oil cans which were carried on the footplate of most of the line's locomotives and the headlamp. This picture also shows clearly the coupling systems and the sizeable spark arrestor.

Superior caught for a moment between shunting operations. The outward appearance of the Bowaters locomotives was greatly improved when no spark arrestor was fitted. Note the usual three oil cans.

10.7.67

Superb was the last of the 0–6–2T Bagnalls supplied to Bowaters, being built in 1940 as works no. 2624. As with most of the locomotives on the railway it was maintained in good condition.

10.7.67

Alpha, with its heavy train loaded with bales, stands in the sidings. Four 0–6–2 tanks built by Bagnalls were operated on the Bowaters system.

10.7.67

Superior was one of the five locomotives built by Kerr Stuart & Co. Ltd of Stoke-on-Trent operating on the Bowaters system. This sturdy locomotive is an 0–6–2T built in 1920, works no. 4034. As can be seen the railway locomotives were well maintained with name and work plates polished.

10.7.67.

An interesting picture showing the rear end of the locomotive *Alpha*. The sliding window to give protection to the crew is clearly shown, together with other details of this 0–6–2 tank built by Bagnalls of Stafford.

10.7.67

Fireless locomotives were found at many locations where sparks or hot coals, etc. could present a major risk. This one is *Unique* and was owned by the Bowaters United Kingdom Pulp & Paper Mills Ltd at the Sittingbourne works. *Unique* was built by W.G. Bagnall Ltd at Stafford in 1923 as works no. 2216.

10.7.67

Bowaters at Sittingbourne operated an extensive 2 ft 6 in gauge rail system throughout the works. Here *Chevallier*, a large Manning Wardle 0–6–2 tank, built in 1915 as works no. 1877, heads a train of the typical wagons used throughout the system. This particular locomotive was purchased from the Admiralty Chattendon & Upnor railway in 1950. *Chevallier* is now in preservation. Note this is one of the few locomotives working without a spark arrestor, also of interest are the dome and safety valves fitted to this locomotive, reminiscent of early practice.

W.G. Bagnall Ltd supplied several new locomotives to the Bowater Paper Mills over the years, one of which was *Conqueror*, works no. 2192, built in 1922. This photograph was taken on 10 July 1967 when *Conqueror*, in immaculate condition, awaits her next duty. Note the spark arrestor chimney which most of the locomotives were fitted with due to the high fire risk.

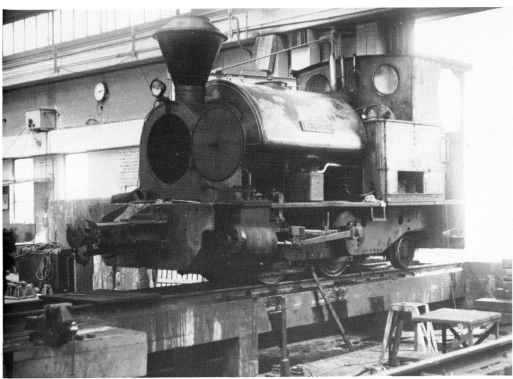

Two of the Bowaters locomotives were built by Kerr Stuart in 1905, *Premier* and *Leader*, the latter receives attention here. The works no. of this locomotive is 926, a few years after building, the engine was rebuilt as was its sister *Premier*.

Melior, a sturdy 0–4–2T, was built in 1924 by Kerr Stuart and supplied new to the Bowaters railway system, where it was one of several 0–4-2Ts in the collection of locomotives. In the photograph the locomotive quietly raises steam for the day's duties.

The Kettering ironstone quarries had 3 ft gauge Manning Wardle 0–6–0STs. *No. 8* was works no. 1675 of 1906 and was supplied new to the line. Here on a very wet November day in 1955 the locomotive crews change over near the engine shed.

Kettering Furnaces No. 7, a veteran Manning Wardle of 1897, works no. 1370. Like its two sisters the engine was supplied new to the line. During its working life it was rebuilt in 1950. Note the wagons and steam crane in the background.

When this photograph was taken on 11 November 1955, this veteran was already seventy-six years old. Black Hawthorn & Co. Ltd built no. 501 in 1879. Kettering ironstone quarries operated three Black Hawthorns at one time, of which no. 501 was the oldest. The last to be supplied, which arrived in 1887 (no. 893) went for scrap in 1927.

For several years this derelict 3 ft gauge De Winton stood overlooking the sea and the main line at Penmaenmawr, North Wales. *Watkin* was built at Caernarvon in 1893, ending its working days in the mid-1940s. The veteran De Winton was photographed in July 1961.

42

The other side of *Watkin* showing that this De Winton was still remarkably intact in 1961, which was surprising since it stood on the line for so many years. The effects of the salt-laden atmosphere and continuous exposure can clearly be seen on the engine. Fortunately this veteran still survives together with two others from the Penmaenmawr quarries.

Metre gauge Peckett 2029 of 1942, shunts at Wellingborough ironworks on 11 November 1955. Three Pecketts were employed at the time on quarry duties, feeding the ironstone straight into the works. All three engines from the quarry system, which was under S&L Minerals ownership in its later days, survive in preservation. Note the standard gauge wagons on the line above the Peckett. Nothing now remains of this sizeable complex. The trains were a familiar and frequent sight crossing the Finedon–Wellingborough road.

Another photograph taken on the S&L Minerals metre gauge system at Wellingborough. Here Peckett no. 1871 of 1934, in its immaculate dark green livery, stands ready for its next turn of duty, note the spark arrestor and central buffer. This line was known to many in its working days as it crossed the Finedon–Wellingborough road.

No. 86, Peckett no. 1871 of 1934, is made ready for another day's work outside the locomotive shed at Wellingborough. In the background some of the tipping wagons used on the line can be seen. The usual method of operation was to have two locomotives in steam, one at the quarry end, either No. 85 or No. 86, with the larger and heavier Peckett working the final section to the furnaces.

Another train of empties rattles past the locomotive depot at Wellingborough on its way back to the quarry, headed by Peckett 1871 of 1934.

A rail tour with a difference. The days of the metre gauge system at Wellingborough, owned at this time by Stewart & Lloyds Ltd, were numbered and several trips were run for enthusiasts. S&L No. 85, Peckett no. 1870, built in 1934, heads the train, banked by No. 87, Peckett no. 2029 of 1942. Both the locomotives were supplied new to the line, together with No. 86 P1871/34 which was also in use at the time. When this photograph was taken the line was the last steam-operated narrow gauge ironstone tramway.

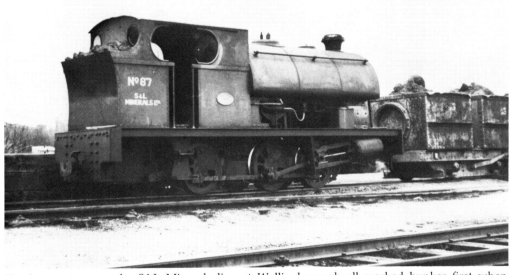

The locomotives on the S&L Minerals line at Wellingborough all worked bunker first when working ore trains to the furnaces. No. 87, the last new locomotive built for this metre gauge line was completed by Pecketts in 1942 and supplied at this time due to increased demand during the Second World War. Usually this locomotive was employed working the trains on the final section into the works themselves.

When this photograph was taken at Gilfach DDU, Llanberis, two of the Padarn Railway Hunslets remained, they are seen here in June 1963 awaiting their fate. The third engine had already been cut up at this time. The locomotives are *Dinorwic* and *Amathaea*, built in 1882 and 1886 respectively.

Another view of one of the Padarn Hunslets. The Padarn Railway was opened in 1848, replacing an earlier 2 ft gauge horse tramway. The line closed in October 1961, road transport then taking over. The workmen's trains which were previously operated over the line stopped running in November 1947.

When the Padarn Railway closed both locomotives were stored at Llanberis. One was to see further service in track lifting during 1962–3, probably the one in this photograph. The original 1848 locomotive, *Fire Queen*, is now preserved at Penrhyn Castle Museum, its sister locomotive *Jenny Lind* was scrapped in 1886. Both were replaced by the Hunslets as seen here. Note the mountainous waste slate tip in the background.

The Padarn Railway transported slate to Port Dinorwic and was being laid to 4 ft gauge. Note the frames of one of the narrow gauge Hunslets, *Lady Madcap*, is to be seen lying next to the locomotive. These frames survived for six years after the larger Hunslet was scrapped in 1963.

The Standard Gauge Industrial Lines

Throughout the British Isles standard gauge industrial steam locomotives were once a familiar sight. In some counties they numbered hundreds, while in others, perhaps without mineral workings or heavy industry,only a few were to be found. Even here, steam often worked at a location such as a sugar beet factory. One fascination for the industrial enthusiast was the wide variety of designs, as most of the locomotive builders constructed engines for private companies. In the period covered by this book many unusual engines had been withdrawn from service, ending their days in a scrap-yard, or even having been cut up on site. If one was lucky on an industrial visit at this time, a real veteran, or unusual design, while not having worked for many years was often to be found dumped at the end of an isolated siding, slowly rusting away.

In view of the large numbers of steam engines in service, it would be impossible to do other than outline the standard gauge locomotives in the space available. Therefore, it has been intended to briefly mention the range and variety, giving most attention to the systems which have been given photographic coverage. I appreciate that many interesting locations and engines have not been mentioned, to those whose favourite system has not been included – my apologies.The various service establishments which had steam power still in use have also been excluded, these are a separate subject in their own right. Several Naval Dockyards, Army and Air Force establishments, were operating their own locomotives many of which were seldom seen by the public, and generally not available to the enthusiast.

Many locomotives at this time were employed on duties at docks, ports and harbour installations throughout the country. At Falmouth, Cornwall, one could quite easily watch the Hawthorn Leslie 0–4–0 saddle tanks at work, from the public road which runs at high level overlooking the docks. In addition to the Hawthorns one solitary Peckett was on site during the 1960s. Moving east along the Cornish coastline to the Port of Par, two very sturdy Bagnalls operated. These Bagnalls were kept in immaculate condition, and were special in that they had cut-down mountings to enable them to pass under the Western Region line. One of the pair was built in 1937, the other, *Alfred*, was almost identical and supplied in 1953, both were supplied new to the line. During the 1950s, a 1927-built Sentinel was on site. It spent many years stored out of use under a tarpaulin, and was perhaps missed by some visitors.

In Hampshire the large dock areas of Southampton were mainly worked by the ex-USA 0–6–0 tanks of the Southern region. However, industrial steam was to be found shunting on wharves in the area, with two Pecketts owned by Southern Wharves Ltd at Dibbles Wharf in steam on most days during the 1950s. In later years, when owned by

Corrall Ltd, the line was worked by an ex-LSWR B4 dock tank, 30096, and a Robert Stephenson & Hawthorn 0–4–0ST, *Bonnie Prince Charlie*, built in 1949. Both of these engines are now in preservation.

The other large dock complex in the West of England was at Avonmouth, operated by the Port of Bristol Authority. Here a sizeable number of Bristol-built Avonside & Peckett locomotives were at work, although even during the 1950s a number of diesels were already in use within the docks, having started to arrive steadily from 1950 onwards. Two of the steam stock have survived into preservation, one of which is still at Bristol. During the mid-1950s the steam collection numbered eighteen engines, the oldest being an interesting Peckett built in 1900.

The Port of London Authority systems, covering the Royal Group of docks – Millwall, Tilbury and West India, all operated steam locomotives, although with mainly diesel locomotives at the Tilbury location. However, nearby at Samuel Williams & Sons Ltd's Dagenham dock, real veterans were still hard at work. For instance, No. 4, a real treasure, built by Manning Wardle of Leeds in 1877. This veteran was maintained in excellent condition until withdrawn from service in 1957, luckily it is still with us in preservation, spending several years at Bressingham Steam Museum in Norfolk until re-located. Several other Manning Wardles were working to the docks during my visit in 1956, but time was already running out for them, as several were laid aside a year later, while the two which had already been withdrawn were standing derelict awaiting their fate, in company with No. 5, a Sentinel similar to those used by LNER. Other than the Manning Wardles, a 1923 Peckett, also an Andrew Barclay of 1907 vintage, and two Hudswell Clarke 0–6–0STs made up the motive power. At the time of my visit several diesels were also operating.

The extensive Manchester Ship Canal rail system was worked by Hudswell Clarkes, Hunslet & Kitson 0–6–0 tank engines, and a few 0–4–0STs built by Pecketts. At Liverpool the Mersey Docks and Harbour Board operated a large number of saddle tanks, most of which were built by Avonside of Bristol. Further north the Ribble Navigation & Preston Dock Undertaking preferred Bagnalls, seven being on the stock list all built 1942–8, with a large 'Fireless', built by Andrew Barclay in 1923. In the north west steam locomotives worked the docks at Workington and Whitehaven. In later years the locomotives employed at Workington Harbour & Dock Co. Ltd, Workington, were all 0–4–0 saddle tanks built by the Yorkshire Engine Co. Ltd between 1947 and 1955. The Seaham Harbour & Dock Co. Ltd at Seaham, County Durham, was famous for the Head Wrightson 0–4–0 vertical boiler locomotives. The real veteran, *Lewin*, an 0–4–0ST dating back to 1863, was still occasionally used, mostly when repair work was undertaken on the Staithes.

Not far away at Sunderland, the Pallion Shipyard owned by William Doxford & Sons Ltd was to become a mecca for enthusiasts, as at this location seven crane tanks were still to be seen. In the 1950s, four or five were in daily use, with the Peckett also at the location being responsible for normal shunting duties. The crane tanks consisted of four built by Robert Stephenson & Hawthorn Ltd between 1940 and 1942, a sole Andrew Barclay built in 1912, and two built by Hawthorn Leslie. The four RSH crane tanks have all been preserved, one of which forms part of the well-known Bressingham collection in Norfolk.

When the first of the new season's crop of sugar beet arrived in late November, early December, or in the case of a bad season, early January rail activity increased. The locomotives owned by the British Sugar Corporation were then certainly kept fully occupied, some having been stored since the end of the previous season. The majority of these beet processing stations are in Eastern England, where the crop is extensively grown, although the company operates processing plants in other parts of the country. At the British Sugar headquarters in Peterborough, the adjoining factory operated two steam locomotives in the 1950s, often assisted by a further engine on hire from British Railways; during one very busy season I can recall a J67 0–6–0 tank being used. Some of the other plants using steam were Spalding in Lincolnshire, Bury St Edmunds and Ipswich in Suffolk, while in Norfolk the Cantley, Lynn & Wissington factories all used locomotives built by various builders. At Wissington the well-known 'Light Railway' was of great interest with its two veteran Manning Wardles of 1901 and 1921 vintage. In the early 1950s a Hudswell Clarke 0–4–0 saddle tank was also stored on site.

Other good hunting grounds for industrial steam were the larger gasworks and electricity generating stations. Many of the gas boards throughout the country operated steam locomotives at their larger works, while others had diesel locomotives. In most cases all one might find were one or two locomotives at a particular site. Many were small 0–4–0 saddle tanks, although some had unusual locomotives, such as the Sentinel which shunted at Cambridge for a great many years having been supplied new to the site in 1929, when it was still a private undertaking. On the outskirts of Edinburgh a number of Andrew Barclays shunted the yards of the large plant at Granton, while up in Aberdeen a 1947 Andrew Barclay, and a veteran Black Hawthorn built way back in 1887, were to be found, the latter carrying the name *City of Aberdeen*. Both engines worked on the docks at times, and were fitted with plating covering the wheels and running gear. If one was lucky one might catch a glimpse of one or two of the Manning Wardle 0–4–2 tanks built in 1915 for the Great North of Scotland Railway (BR class Z4 and Z5) working on the docks. These locomotives carried BR nos 68190, '91, '92, '93.

One of the largest steam operations run by the Central Electricity Generating Board was at Hams Hall Generating Station, situated at Coleshill, Warwickshire, where in later years seven RSH 0–6–0 tanks, together with two Peckett 0–4–0 saddle tanks, and a sole Hawthorn Leslie, provided the motive power. These locomotives will be remembered as being in fine condition. On most days a visitor would usually find six or seven engines in operation, with a smaller number operating at weekends.

Other Midlands generating stations which operated steam into the 1960s were at Castle Donnington, Coventry, Ironbridge and Leicester. The new power station built at Goldington near Bedford was supplied with two new Andrew Barclay saddle tanks, resplendent in dark blue livery. No more than ten miles away the Little Barford station had two more Barclays, usually with one in steam daily. Throughout the country many other generating stations had steam locomotives in daily use to handle the incoming coal supplies. In fact, quite a number of new industrial steam locomotives were supplied to the CEGB during the early and mid-1950s, and like their main line counterparts they had a comparatively short working life.

Engines of various mineral lines provided a fascinating variety of designs. The Oxfordshire Ironstone Co. Ltd was to be found at Wroxton near Banbury, having an extensive number of locomotives, operating from three locomotive sheds. Most of the engines have been supplied new to the system. During the 1950s visitors could see several of the locomotives active daily. Some of them were supplied as recently as 1952–3, while a Sentinel was one of the last engines to arrive, being supplied new in 1956. Later years were to see several locomotives from the system among the BR engines awaiting their fate in Cohen's scrap-yard in Kettering.

In adjoining Northamptonshire many ironstone quarries were still active in the 1950s and '60s, and by far the largest was the extensive Stewart & Lloyds Minerals system. Engines working from their new depot at Pen Green, operational from August 1954, having previously worked from Corby shed. Several veteran Manning Wardles, powerful Kitson 0–6–0 saddle tanks, several Robert Stephenson & Hawthorn 0–6–0 saddle tanks of the 'Austerity' design, and a solitary Hudswell Clarke, No. 35, *Rhos*, made up the full complement. All the locomotives, resplendent in their dark green livery, were maintained in excellent condition. Not many miles away from Corby, the South Durham Steel & Iron Company operated at Irchester and Storefield. Here a selection of veterans were to be found, while a row of derelicts were slowly rusting away. The furthest east in the county that ironstone was quarried was at Cranford where Staveley Minerals Ltd operated with an Avonside and two Bagnalls, the latter specially built for ironstone duties in 1942. This quarry remained open until quite late in the period, dispatching the iron ore to Kettering and the Midland mainline via the remaining section of the Kettering–Huntingdon line.

Several other mineral systems were still operational, some having steam in service, plus the narrow and metre gauge lines . Other systems which were still operational were the S&L Minerals lines at Desborough and Glendon. In the north-east corner of Northamptonshire the Nassington and Barrowden Mining Co. Ltd were operating two Hunslet 0–6–0 saddle tanks, having a Peckett stored outside. The two Hunslets are now in use on preserved lines, one at the nearby Nene Valley Railway, the other on the North Norfolk Railway at Sheringham.

Another important ironstone county was Lincolnshire, where S&L Minerals had quarry systems at Harlaxton, also nearby in Leicestershire, at Market Overton, Pilton and Harston. At Harlaxton the locomotives included two 0–6–0 tanks, *Ajax* – an Andrew Barclay of 1918 vintage, and the powerful *Harlaxton* built by the same company in 1941. In addition to the above also at this location, were several 0–6–0 saddle tanks built by a number of different engine builders.

Considerable numbers of industrial steam locomotives were employed at the various steelworks throughout the country. One of the largest was the gigantic Stewart & Lloyds complex at Corby. In addition furnaces at nearby Wellingborough and Kettering were operational, these being among the earliest to close in the 1950s. Other steelworks using steam were to be found at Etruria in Staffordshire, notable for the Dubs Crane Tanks.

In Derbyshire, Stanton & Stavely had a crane tank operating at Alfreton. Other works belonging to this company were to be found at Holwell near Melton Mowbray, Leicestershire, and the Stanton Ironworks near Ilkeston, Derbyshire. Further north the massive Appleby Frodingham Steel Company operated a large number of steam locomotives, while other large steelworks were to be found in South and North Wales and Cumberland. Visitors to the huge Corby steelworks were amazed at the rail activity; numerous engines shunting in the works yards, others disposing of waste products, while others were responsible for handling wagons of steel tube which was being despatched over the BR network. In addition Messrs Shanks & McEwan even had two of their own locomotives (both real veterans incidentally) handling waste materials. The modern locomotive depot maintained the S&L fleet well, both mechanically and externally. As will be seen from the photographs many real veterans were still active and in daily use.

The National Coal Board operated a vast number of steam locomotives, which could become the subject of a book in themselves. Their locomotive stock was extremely varied, most of the major builders being represented, together with locomotives purchased from the mainline companies, some of the ex-mainline pre-grouping survivors were still active in the early 1960s. Many other locomotives were purchased for use at collieries as steam was withdrawn on British Railways.

Numerous other private companies operated their own steam locomotives, including motor car manufacturers, breweries, chemical works and paper mills to name just a few. Other quarry lines where steam was to be found existed, including gypsum, granite and clay.

Central Electricity Generating Board ED10 at Goldington power-station. This Andrew Barclay no. 2354 was built in 1954, when two identical locomotives were supplied new to the site. Here ED10, now named *Richard Trevithick*, awaits its next duty.

28.9.69

Many Central Electricity Board generating stations operated steam locomotives. A considerable number were built by Andrew Barclay, Kilmarnock, as was no. 2069, built in 1939 and named *Little Barford*. This engine was engaged in duties at the Bedfordshire power-station of that name on 22 November 1954.

One of the Central Electricity Board's Andrew Barclays, *Edmundsons*, was photographed at Little Barford. This stocky 0–4–0ST was built at Kilmarnock in 1943 as works no. 2168. This power-station has been closed and dismantled, although discussions have been taking place with a view to building a new generating station on the site. Rail traffic is still worked to the old reception sidings, not with coal as previously but fly ash from Midlands power-stations, and used by a company on an adjacent site.

The other one of the two brand new Andrew Barclay 0–4–0 saddle tanks which were supplied to the Central Electricity Generating Board at Goldington power-station, Bedford, in 1954. Here AB 2352/54, (ED9) shunts building materials while its sister AB 2354/54 (ED10) stands nearby.

30.10 54

This Peckett design dated from the turn of the century. Peckett no. 808 was built in 1900 and supplied new to the Port of Bristol Authority. All steam locomotives of the PBA were Pecketts or Avonsides. The engine carries the nameplate *Kenneth* and was photographed on 9 September 1956.

The Port of Bristol Authority at Avonmouth Docks operated a considerable number of steam locomotives during the 1950s before the arrival of diesels. However, *Edward*'s working days were over when photographed in September 1956, having been withdrawn from service two years earlier. The locomotive is Peckett 1377/14.

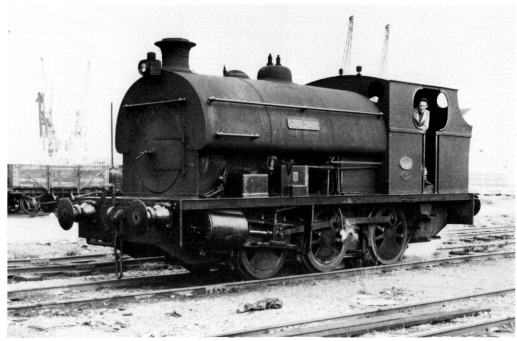

Peckett & Sons Ltd of Bristol built this sturdy 0–6–0ST in 1943. Three consecutively numbered locomotives were supplied new to the Port of Bristol Authority Avonmouth docks, not far from the engine's 'birthplace'. The photograph is of *Clifton*, works no. 2037, and was taken during a pause in shunting operations on 8 September 1956.

Alfred, one of the Avonsides at the Port of Bristol Authority Avonmouth docks. The engine was works no. 1679 of 1914. Like most of the locomotives at the location it was supplied new. Many steam engines were still at work here in 1956, even though diesels had been on site since 1950, others arriving in 1955–6.

PBA Avonmouth *Henbury*, a Peckett of 1937, works no. 1940. This engine is very similar in design to the locomotives supplied several years later by this company. As can be seen the locomotive was in steam, and ready to leave the shed for its next turn of duty.

With steam leaking from several places, Kerr Stuart 3063/18 shunts in the yards of Fairfields shipyard at Chepstow on 25 October 1965. Also at this location was an ex-Great Eastern Y5, built by Neilsons in 1876. Both the engines from Fairfields have been preserved.

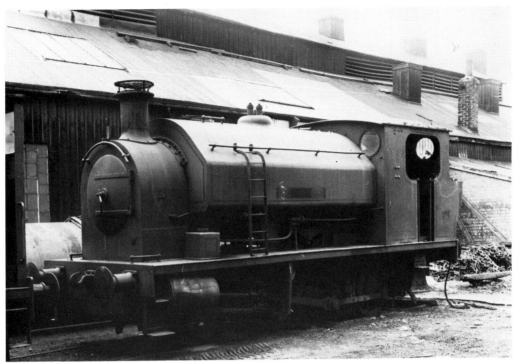

Ribble Navigation & Preston Docks Undertaking, Bagnall 0–6–0ST, no. 2893 of 1948, carried the name *Conqueror* although it had lost both its name and works plate, when this photograph was taken on a gloomy March day in 1968.

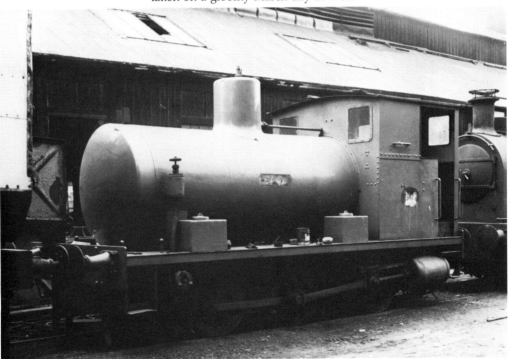

Duke, an 0–6–0 fireless locomotive, also belonged to the Ribble Navigation Company at Preston docks. This engine was built by Andrew Barclay in 1927. Here again note the missing name and work plates at this time.

Two Manning Wardles stand awaiting the next sugar beet season, at the Wissington factory on 8 May 1954. On the left is *Newcastle*, MW 1532/01, and on the right MW 2006/21. Exposure to the elements did little to help the external condition of the Manning Wardles.

Very few industrial steam locomotives were to be found in the county of Norfolk, most of those that were there were to be found at systems involving sugar beet. One location was the Wissington Light Railway. On 8 May 1954 this Hudswell Clarke, works no. 533, built in 1899 was stored, being sold to a dealer and scrapped not many months after this photograph was taken.

The locomotive crews chat, while Avonside 1945/26 awaits its next turn of duty at the British Sugar Corporation's Woodston factory, Peterborough, on 4 December 1954. During the 1954 season three locomotives were in use, one a J67 on loan from British Railways.

Newcastle, a veteran Manning Wardle built in 1901, on the Wissington Light Railway stands by the water tank. During the spring and summer the locomotive saw little use. *Newcastle* was MW works no. 1532. This photograph was taken on 8 May 1954, a bright spring day.

Hudswell Clarke 1800/47 is well-known to many children as *Thomas* in preservation. Here the engine is seen in British Sugar Corporation service at Peterborough in December 1954. During the height of the sugar beet season at least three locomotives would be in daily use. At this time a J67, usually from Stratford shed, could be found working here also.

Another view of Peckett no. 1703, this time showing the other side of the engine. Pecketts were among the most popular of the builders of industrial locomotives; engines built at the Atlas Locomotive Works were to be found in many parts of the world.

4.6.66

Having completed its duties for the day, Peckett no. 1703 of 1926, *Langar*, simmers gently at the cement works of G.T. Earl Ltd, Barnston, on 4 June 1966.

Immaculate in its dark green livery this sturdy Avonside 1875/21 was caught by the camera during its shunting duties on a sunny April day in 1969. The engine was owned by the Rugby Cement Company, and operated at its Barrington works in Cambridgeshire.

Park Gate Iron & Steel Co. Ltd No. 8, an interesting locomotive built by the Yorkshire Engine Company in 1905, as works no. 784. When caught by the camera on a sunny November day in 1954, No. 8 was in immaculate condition at the Charwelton ironstone quarries, Northamptonshire.

The standard British Railways ore wagon almost dwarfs Yorkshire Engine Co. works no. 784. This engine was a typical example of how many industrial locomotives were to be found during the 1950s, the driver taking great pride in maintaining his engine in good condition. Note the No. 8 carried on the chimney. Very few industrials built by the Yorkshire Engine Co. are in preservation.

For many years this Sentinel was a familiar sight shunting at the Eastern Gas Board, Coldhams Lane, Cambridge. It was supplied new in 1929, being Sentinel works no. 8024. The locomotive had a good head of steam when photographed on 9 May 1955. The locomotive is now in preservation. Note the chain drive, clearly seen in this photograph.

Another view of Sentinel 8024 showing the other side of the locomotive. As can be seen the chain drive was on one side of the engine only. This interesting Sentinel worked for many years at Coldhams Lane, Cambridge.

The third photograph of the Eastern Gas Board's Sentinel shows the cab clearly. The famous Sentinel works plate can be seen on the cab side. Note the firebox, and chimney going up and through the cab roof.

During the 1950s the South Western Gas Board had two Peckett locomotives at Exeter gasworks. This one is works no. 2074 supplied new by Peckett & Sons Ltd's Atlas Locomotive Works, Bristol, in 1946. It was photographed in fine condition during September 1956.

A grimy Andrew Barclay at work in the yards of Granton gasworks, Edinburgh. AB no. 1967/35 was one of the Barclays employed at this location.

City of Aberdeen, a real veteran built in 1887 by Black Hawthorn & Co. Ltd (works no. 912), was still in regular use when photographed at Aberdeen gasworks on 24 August 1955. Note the supports for plating to cover the wheels when working on the dockside. This interesting veteran is preserved in Scotland, at the Scottish RPS depot.

Not all the locomotives on the Bowaters Paper Mills railway at Sittingbourne were narrow gauge, as they also operated two standard gauge locomotives on the Ridham dock. One of these was an ex-SECR 'P' class 0–6–0 tank built at Ashford works in 1910. Ending its BR days as 31178 in 1958. This engine is now one of the three 'P' class locomotives on the Bluebell Railway.

Aberdeen gasworks also owned this Andrew Barclay 2239 of 1947, seen here on the dockside, next to a typical car of this period. The engine was fitted with covers over the wheels and motion for safety reasons when working in areas such as this. The Barclay was in blue livery with white lining when photographed on 24 August 1955. This engine has survived into preservation.

The other standard gauge locomotive at Ridham Docks was this powerful Bagnall saddle tank, *Jubilee*, built in 1936 as works no. 2542, photographed on 10 July 1967. This locomotive is now in preservation at the Stour Valley Railway.

Pioneer II, the ex-SECR 'P' class tank pauses from its shunting duties at Ridham dock. Two standard gauge steam locomotives were owned by Bowaters Paper Mills and worked at this location.
10.7.67

National Coal Board Opencast Executive operated this Hudswell Clarke 0–4-0ST works no. 1727 of 1941. Photographed at Crigglestone in Yorkshire on 20 March 1966.

The National Coal Board were also the owners of this sturdy Hudswell Clarke 0–6–0ST No. 31, built in 1955, as works no. 1881. Here the locomotive awaits its next turn of duty at the Park Hall Colliery.

Bickershaw, a Hunslet built in 1933, carried the No. 42, here the locomotive stands out of use at Park Hall Colliery in the Wakefield area. Note the unusual chimney. This engine was photographed on 20 March 1966, and scrapped two months later.

Several Hunslets of this design were to be found in various parts of the country. This one, Hunslet 1725/35 *Jubilee*, was busy at Newmarket Silkstone Colliery, one of the NCB Castleford area pits on 20 March 1966.

A typical Peckett 0–4-0ST photographed on a grey November day in 1955, at the Southern Wharves rail system, Northam, Southampton. The locomotive is no. 1638, built in 1923, and named *Bristol*. The engine was supplied via Pecketts in 1935, having previously been at Barnsley gasworks.

The well-maintained engine of the Chapel Tramway Company Ltd, Southampton, stands outside the small locomotive shed in light steam on 9 November 1955. Peckett 1375 was built in 1914 and supplied new. Note the solid square buffers fitted to the locomotive, common on many industrial engines.

This Bagnall saddle tank was built at Stafford in 1953 as works no. 3058. It was supplied new for duties at Par harbour in Cornwall, where a similar locomotive had been supplied in 1937. *Alfred* was caught by the camera during a lunch break on 5 September 1956, after just three years of service.

Marks on the tank side show where the nameplate *Bombay* was fitted to Samuel Williams No. 8. This Manning Wardle 1674 of 1906 came to Dagenham in 1932, going for scrap with two other locomotives in 1957.

This typical Peckett design was the only locomotive built by this company on the rail system of Samuel Williams. Two other companies had owned *Maryhill*, before it reached Dagenham, where it is pictured here, just before the outbreak of the Second World War. The locomotive was Peckett 1606/23.

Hudswell Clarke & Co. Ltd built this locomotive in 1937. It was the most modern locomotive in the list of steam engines employed by Samuel Williams, joining the company from McAlpines three years after construction. The engine's works no. was 1676.

Andrew Barclay 0–4–0ST no. 1129 of 1907 came to Samuel Williams from Scotland in 1940, becoming No. 12. Here the locomotive carries out shunting duties in a typical dockland setting. Note the spark arrestor which all Samuel Williams locomotives carried.

Surprisingly Samuel Williams No. 3 *Edgware*, with brasswork shining, was only a year away from being withdrawn from service when photographed. Several Manning Wardles were employed at this location, this one, no. 2049, built in 1926, was the youngest example.

Years of lying derelict and exposed to the elements had certainly taken their toll on this Sentinel, works no. 5735. It had been supplied new to Samuel Williams in 1926. The engine is a four wheel geared drive with vertical boiler similar to the engines used on the LNER and elsewhere. No. 5 ended its days being sold for scrap to Messrs Cohens in 1957. Note the long since faded paintwork and rust in the cab side sheets.

No. 9, its working days over, awaits its fate. This Manning Wardle was built in 1903 as works no. 1617. In 1922, during the course of its working life, it was rebuilt by the Yorkshire Engine Co. When this photograph was taken on 24 May 1956, it was only a matter of months before this engine, with others, was sold for scrap to Messrs Cohens.

The crew of veteran Manning Wardle no. 641 of 1877 kindly stopped the locomotive to enable me to take this photograph after its day's duties had finished at Samuel Williams & Sons Ltd, Dagenham docks on 24 May 1956. The locomotive was within a year of being withdrawn from service, initially to be preserved by the company and later by the railway preservation movement. Note the safety valve cover cab, wooden buffers and front brake blocks.

Samuel Williams No. 7, another of the Manning Wardles, in this case works no. 1488, built in 1900. This engine came from a company in Caerphilly, South Wales in 1929. The locomotive was here being prepared for another round of duty in the docks. On most days in the mid-1950s five or more locomotives were regularly in steam.

Very few locomotives were supplied new to Dagenham docks. This Manning Wardle, *Edgware*, carried the number 3, (an earlier No. 3 being scrapped in 1947). *Edgware* came to the site via a London based contractor in 1936. This particular locomotive was built at Hunslet, Leeds, in 1926 as works no. 2045. The engine was nearing the end of its working life when this photograph was taken, as just over a year later it was derelict. Note the rail steam crane behind No. 3.

24.5.56

The gem of the Samuel Williams locomotives, No. 4, Manning Wardle 641 of 1877, stands outside the small locomotive depot. Note the two steam cranes in the background, items of industrial equipment which received very little attention from steam enthusiasts in the 1950s, when they were still a comparatively common sight.

24.5.56

A preservationist's dream! At Dagenham docks three very interesting locomotives lie derelict awaiting their fate. Today they would be quickly snapped up. Nearest to the camera is No. 5 Sentinel 4WTG no. 5735, supplied new in 1926. Next in line is Manning Wardle 1617/03, and standing on its own is No. 8 *Bombay* Manning Wardle 1674 of 1906. Unfortunately none of these veterans were rescued by preservationists.

24.5.56

This picture clearly shows the problems encountered on some industrial sites when trying to photograph locomotives. No. 1 was built by Manning Wardle of Leeds in 1903, coming to Dagenham docks from a Doncaster contractor in 1934. The works no. of this veteran was 1590. Manning Wardles were very popular on this system. Note the shining brass works plate. No. 1 was the spare engine at this time.

24.5.56

Their day's work done, No. 10, Hudswell Clarke 1526 of 1924, and the veteran No. 4, Manning Wardle 641 of 1877, stand outside the small locomotives depot. No. 10 came from MacAlpines in 1940 and was withdrawn from service in 1957.

24.5.56

This picture shows the veteran No. 4 in a different location. As can be seen, the end of the day's working was near, No. 4 was being coaled up while other locomotives also come on shed.

24.5.56

This, the final picture of the Samuel Williams locomotives, is an interesting view of No. 15, Hudswell Clarke & Co. Ltd, no. 1676 of 1937. All the locomotives at Dagenham were maintained in excellent condition with shining brasswork, making it one of the best locations to visit in the 1950s.

24.5.56

After the end of the sugar beet season the locomotives of Wissington Light Railway were left where they finished work until the autumn, when the system became a hive of activity once again. In this photograph are two Manning Wardles, no. 1532 *Newcastle* on the right and no. 2006 on the left, built in 1901 and 1921 respectively.

8.5.54

One of the last ironstone quarry railways operating steam locomotives was the Nassington Barrowden Mining Co. Ltd at Nassington in Northamptonshire. Two Hunslets operated the line up to the end, with a Peckett stored out of use. Here 1953/39 *Jacks Green*, named after a local spinney, is nearest the camera with *Ring Haw* in the background. Both the Hunslets are in preservation, *Jacks Green* on the Nene Valley Railway, *Ring Haw* on the North Norfolk Railway.

19.3.67

Buccleuch was built by Pecketts of Bristol as no. 1232 in 1910. After years on ironstone lines it ended its days at the Nassington & Barrowden Mining Co. Here the locomotive stands out of use awaiting its fate, which was unfortunately the scrap man's cutting torch.

Another photograph of *Buccleuch*, an example of one of the larger Peckett saddle tank designs. Note the safety valves fitted to this locomotive, typical of early locomotive practice, also the water gauge fitted to the front of the saddle tank.

19.3.67

The cramped conditions of the locomotive shed at Bath gasworks, made photography of the locomotives very difficult as neither was in steam. The engine against the buffers is Peckett no. 1267, built in 1919, and the other in the background is Avonside no. 1978 of 1928.

31.8.55

Bath gasworks' Avonside 0–4–0ST no. 1978 was built in 1928 and is photographed here in the cramped shed surroundings. Only two locomotives were employed at this location, both Bristol-built engines, as the other was a Peckett 0–4–0ST.

31.8.55

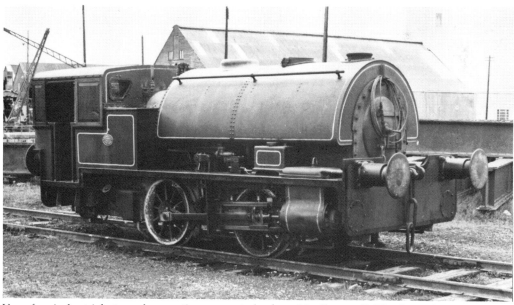

Very few industrial steam locomotives were to be found in Cornwall. The Port of Par Ltd at Par harbour had three in the 1950s, two of which, Bagnall 0–4–0STs, were in regular use. The third engine, a Sentinel, was in the yard under a tarpaulin. The two Bagnalls were of identical design although built sixteen years apart. In order to enable them to get under a low bridge they were of cut-down construction.. This one, the oldest, is works no. 2572, built in 1937.

6.5.56

Another view of the Port of Par Bagnall, *Alfred*, built in 1953 and supplied new to the system. Note the stepped down footplate and cut-down chimney on this powerful looking locomotive.

6.9.56

Shining like a new pin and resplendent in its dark blue livery, Andrew Barclay no. 2354 of 1954, had just been delivered to the new Goldington power-station and had yet to be commissioned. The other new Barclay was already employed on moving construction materials on site.

30.10.54

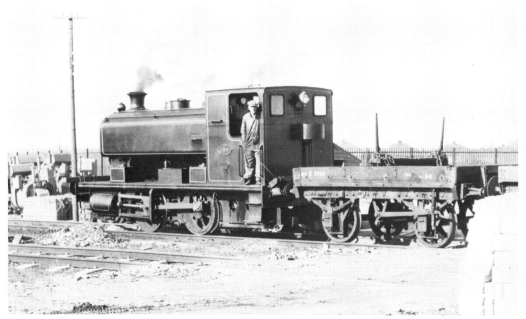

ED9, Andrew Barclay 2352 of 1954, at work shunting materials at Goldington power-station. Locomotives built by Barclays were very popular with the generating stations. Note the 'match truck' often used when steel or similar materials were transported by rail to allow for any overhang of the load.

30.10.54

One could often find locomotives in a state such as this, perhaps an engine would be dismantled and found to be beyond economical repair, or parts were needed to keep another in service. Photographed here at the South Durham Irchester quarries are the remains of Avonside no. 1787/17.

20.1.66

A row of derelict locomotives were dumped on a siding at Irchester, Northants, for several years. Among those locomotives was this Peckett no. 1258, built in 1912, and originally named *Rothwell*. Note the early pattern of safety valves fitted. The locomotives were all from the South Durham Steel & Iron Co. Ltd., Irchester quarry.

2.5.56

A long time had elapsed since this Andrew Barclay 0–4–0ST was in steam. Built in 1914, its works no. was 1363, and it carried the name *Major*. This locomotive came to the South Durham system at Irchester from West Hartlepool in 1957; just nine years later it was derelict.

22.5.66

This Andrew Barclay also came to Irchester from West Hartlepool, this time in 1959. During the late 1950s and '60s several locomotives were transferred to the site, some soon to end up derelict, as in this case. The locomotive works no. is 1609 and the engine was built in 1918. The plate on the cab-side reads 'South Durham Steel and Iron Co. Ltd, 1918', but the works plate had disappeared.

2.5.66

Also 'out to grass' was this powerful Hawthorn Leslie 0–4–0ST no. 3892, built in 1936, which was one of the two new Hawthorn Leslie locomotives supplied to Irchester quarries. All plates had long since gone from this engine when photographed.

22.5.66

Also standing at Irchester was this steam shovel built by Rustons of Lincoln. Very few enthusiasts would have given this a second look, as at the time equipment of this nature was still commonplace. In the distance can be seen the row of derelict locomotives.

22.5.66

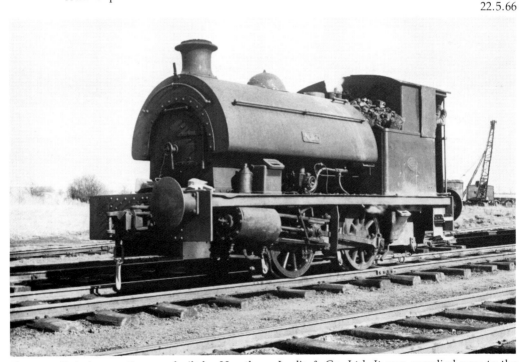

This neat little locomotive was built by Hawthorn Leslie & Co. Ltd. It was supplied new to the Irchester quarries where it was photographed on 16 March 1967. It is HL 3946/37 and carries the plate No. 17. Note the driver's boots just visible at the back of the cab as he has a midday break! The engine has a good head of steam and a plentiful supply of coal in front of the cab.

Locomotives were often transferred from one quarry system to another. In this case Andrew Barclay 2323/52 had recently been transferred into Irchester quarries when caught by the camera. Note it was already minus its name and works plates, and in a deplorable condition.

16.3.67

Occasionally things went wrong, here there are problems with No. 14. Derailments were certainly not unknown on the quarry lines. Manning Wardle No. 14 of the South Durham Irchester system had just derailed itself. The locomotive still had a good head of steam and was quickly rerailed with the aid of jacks. Locomotive details are MW 1795/12, rebuilt by Ridley Shaw in 1936.

3.8.67

Stewart & Lloyds Ltd operated an extensive system of quarry lines. The locomotive here is No. 50 *Carmarthen*, a Kitson-built saddle tank constructed in 1936, photographed while shunting mineral wagons at Glendon East Quarry on 25 April 1967. Several locomotives of this type were to be found at ironstone quarries owned by the company in Northamptonshire.

Its day's duties done, *Carmarthen* heads for home. Note the well-maintained condition of the locomotive, with polished name-, works and numberplates. Unfortunately, this locomotive has not survived into preservation.

S&L Minerals No. 49, *Caerphilly*, another example of the Kitson 0–6-0ST design, shunts loaded ore wagons ready for despatch on 30 March 1967. The locomotive is works no. 5477 of 1936. As with many of the quarry locomotives this engine had worked in the steelworks previously.

In many areas of Northamptonshire industrial engines could be found quietly going about their duties, such as the scene where No. 11, Andrew Barclay 1047/05, shunts mineral wagons on the Storefield quarry system. This locomotive is one of the fortunate ones to survive into preservation.

The early spring sunshine highlights No. 11 at the Storefield ironstone quarry in Northamptonshire. The locomotive No. 11 is Andrew Barclay 1047 of 1905, and is working a train of loaded ore wagons to the railhead. During its working life the Andrew Barclay was rebuilt at the nearby Irchester workshop.

16.3.67

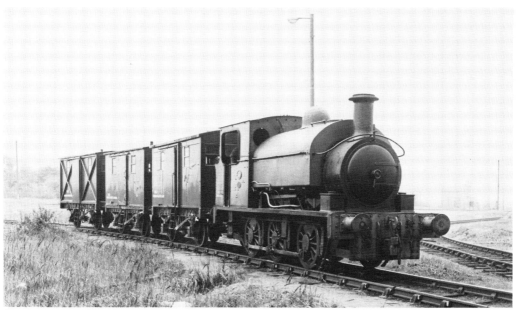

Stewart & Lloyds Ltd ran a very interesting rail tour over a considerable area of the Corby quarry systems on 22 May 1965, using veteran Manning Wardle no. 1317, built in 1895. Here the locomotive stands ready at the head of the special train comprising of three vans.

Another view of the S&L special in a quarry dwarfed by a gigantic dragline, which was one of the landmarks in the area at the time. On most working days during this period approximately sixteen steam locomotives were in use on various parts of the Corby quarry system. All the working locomotives were maintained in good mechanical and external condition.

Only one Hudswell Clarke 0–6–0ST was operated by the Corby quarries, here No. 39, *Rhos*, built in 1918 as works no. 1308 stands at Pen Green. Note the headlight and toolboxes fitted to this sturdy locomotive. This engine has survived into preservation.

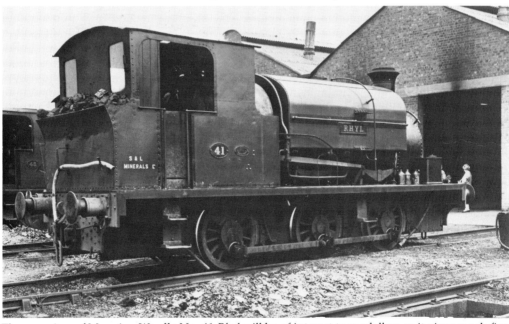

The rear view of Manning Wardle No. 41 *Rhyl* will be of interest to modellers as it gives much fine detail of one of the last designs by this company. The modern Pen Green locomotive depot from which the quarry locomotives operated from 1954 onwards can be seen in the background. The depot was equipped with inspection pits and many other facilities for the maintenance of a fleet of locomotives.

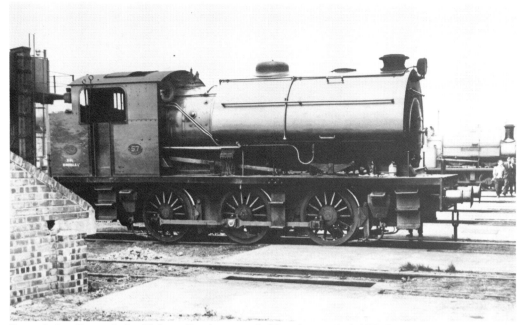

One of the fleet of the Robert Stephenson & Hawthorns 0–6–0ST design operated by S&L Minerals, No. 57, here in spotless condition, was built in 1950 as works no. 7668. Fortunately, this powerful engine is still with us on the Keighley & Worth Valley Railway.

S&L Minerals No. 45, *Colwyn*, was one of the number of Kitsons operated by the company at Corby and elsewhere. This locomotive was works no. 5470 built in 1933. The locomotive was in immaculate S&L Minerals Ltd dark green livery. Several of the Kitsons have survived into preservation including *Colwyn*.

The day's work for Avonside works no. 1919, built in 1924, was over. The locomotive was preparing to go on shed for servicing, but not before a willing driver stopped the locomotive to enable this photograph to be taken. The Cranford quarry was among the last ironstone systems in operation.

23.3.67

In order to work the heavy ironstone trains out of a quarry where steep inclines were often to be found, a charge at the bank was usually necessitated, as was the case at Cranford where the line ran under the Huntingdon to Kettering road. Here *Cranford No. 2* starts out on the run to the reception sidings.

The locomotives at Cranford ironstone quarry, situated near Kettering, Northamptonshire, were usually kept in good external condition. In its last working days the line received many visitors. Here *Cranford No. 2*, Bagnall 2668 of 1942, heads a train of empty tipping wagons back to the quarry. This fine example of Bagnall's 0–6–0ST design has survived into preservation.

Cranford quarries was one of the last working ironstone systems in Northamptonshire, and in later years was owned by Stavely Minerals Ltd. On most days two locomotives could be found in steam, the loaded wagons being sent out via the branch line to Kettering. This sturdy Bagnall 0–6–0ST *Cranford No. 2* was supplied new in 1942, works no. 2668.

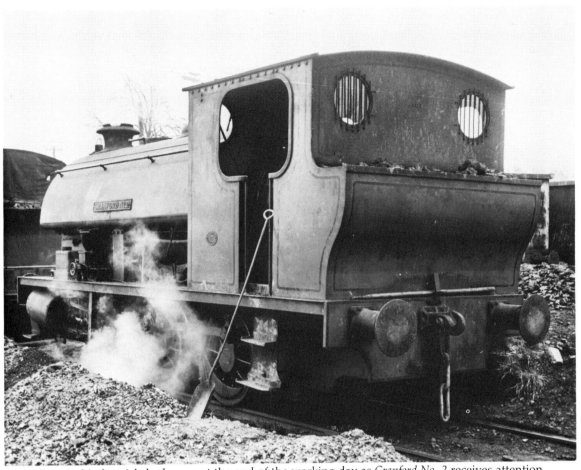

A typical industrial shed scene at the end of the working day as *Cranford No. 2* receives attention. In many instances quarry locomotives were often back on shed for maintenance work in the late afternoon, ready for an early start the next day. This scene shows the usual pile of hot ashes as the locomotive's fire is cleaned.

On 6 May 1965 both locomotives of the Cranford ironstone system were at work. Here Avonside no. 1919 of 1924, *Cranford*, awaits its next turn of duty, note the chimney fitted which does little to improve the looks of this otherwise neat and sturdy design.

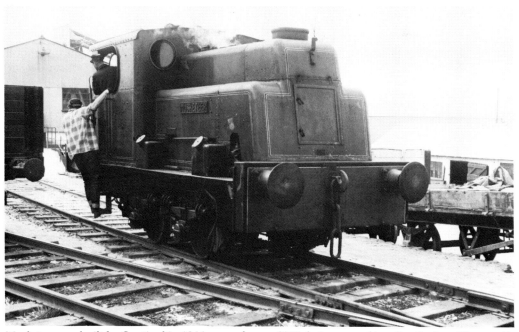

Musketeer was built by Sentinel in 1946 as works no. 9369, being one of two Sentinels at Thomas E. Gray Ltd, Burton Latimer, Northamptonshire. This locomotive was purchased by the company from Coatbridge. The locomotive is pictured here on shunting duties in the works yard on 30 March 1967. This interesting locomotive is a four-wheel tank geared vertical boiler design.

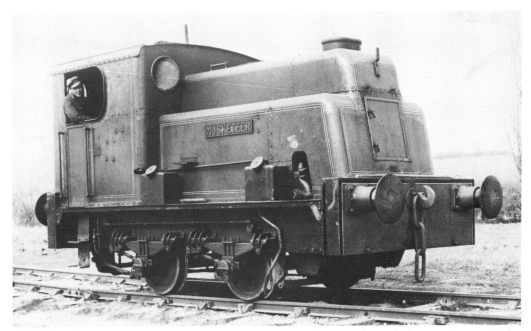

The neat design of Sentinel no. 9369 is clearly seen in this photograph, as the locomotive stands for a moment during shunting operations at Burton Latimer. Note the lining and clean condition. On most days both of the Sentinel locomotives were in use, while a third and much earlier engine built by the company had stood disused for some years. Fortunately, both the later Sentinels, *Musketeer* and *Belvedere*, are preserved.

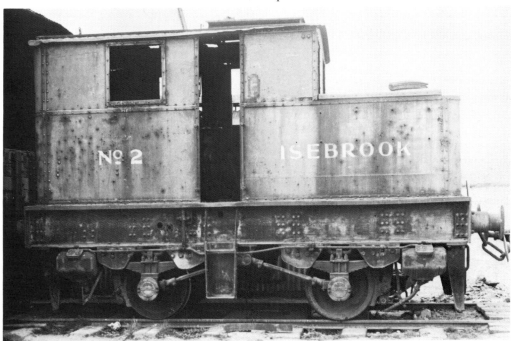

Sentinel 4WTG no. 6515 built in 1926, was originally owned by the Great Western Railway, as No. 12. After a short time it was returned to Sentinels and resold to Messrs Thos. Gray Ltd of Isebrook Quarry, Burton Latimer, Northamptonshire. It was operated here for several years until the arrival of two later Sentinels. It was still on site, disused, on 30 March 1967. No. 2 *Isebrook* has survived into preservation, and is at the present time at the Buckinghamshire Railway Centre.

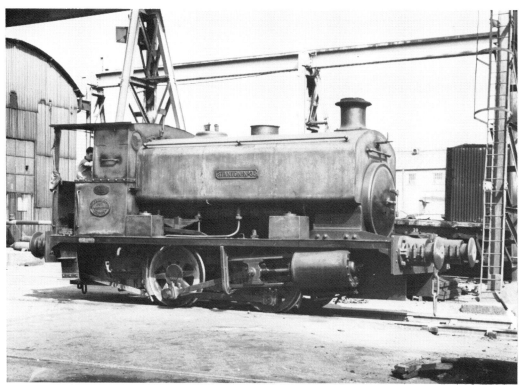

Four of the steam locomotives employed at Stanton & Staveley Ltd's Holwell Ironworks near Melton Mowbray, Leicestershire, were Andrew Barclays. Here *Stanton No. 36*, an 0–4–0ST was busy shunting when photographed on 4 June 1966. The engine is AB 2042/37.

Holwell No. 18 is a typical example of the Andrew Barclay 0–4–0ST design, in this case built in 1923 as works no. 1791. The cylinder cover shows signs of collision damage.

Years of hard work had taken its toll on the chimney of Andrew Barclay no. 1791 of 1923, one of the locomotives at Stanton & Staveley's Holwell ironworks, when it was photographed on 4 June 1966.

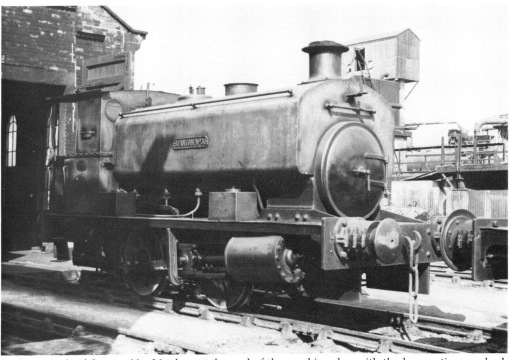

A photograph of *Stanton No. 36* taken at the end of the working day with the locomotive on shed. Stanton & Staveley Ltd had a considerable number of Andrew Barclay 0–4–0STs in their locomotive fleets. These were in service at Holwell, Stanton and Alfreton at this time.

Several ironstone quarries operated by Stewart & Lloyds Minerals Ltd were to be found in counties other than Northamptonshire. One still operating in the mid-1960s was the Buckminster quarry in Lincolnshire where *Stainby*, Andrew Barclay 0–6–0ST no. 2313, built in 1951, was to be found. Note the rear cab window guards and yellow warning panel on the coal bunker.

The steeply graded system at Stewart & Lloyds' Harlaxton quarries was operated by two Andrew Barclay side tanks. The oldest was this impressive 0–6–0T, works no. 1605/18, *Ajax*, photographed 4 June 1966.

Harlaxton was the other Andrew Barclay side tank at the quarries of that name and under works no. 2107 was built during the Second World War and supplied new in 1941. The locomotive was coaling up for its next turn of duty. Both *Harlaxton* and *Ajax* are in preservation.

Also at S&L Minerals Ltd's Harlaxton quarry was *Rutland*, a large 0–6–0ST built by Andrew Barclays in 1954 as works no. 2351. The Harlaxton system usually required four locomotives in steam daily during the 1960s. Operations were difficult with a steep gradient, and mid-way reversing point.

4.6.66

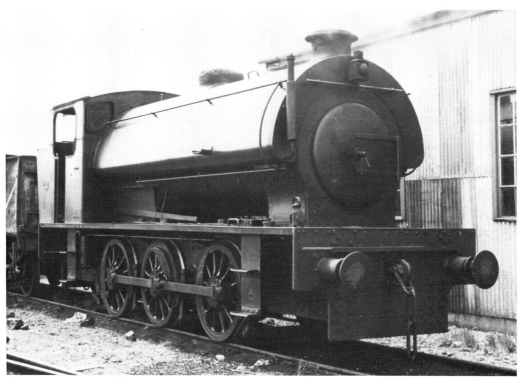

Three modern 0–6–0STs were in the locomotive fleet at Harlaxton, two built by Hunslets in 1941, and the third being a Robert Stephenson & Hawthorns Co. Ltd design. Note the water gauge fitted to the saddle tank.

It looked as if time had almost run out for No. 51, which stood out of use and neglected at Harlaxton quarries in 1966. This Robert Stephenson & Hawthorn 0–6–0ST, works no. 7003, was built in 1940, although first impressions might indicate an older locomotive. No. 51 had been transferred from S&L at Corby.

South Durham Iron & Steel Co. Ltd veteran, 0–4–0ST Manning Wardle No. 14, was built in 1912 as works no. 1795, undergoing rebuilding during its working life. When this photograph was taken in March 1966 the working locomotives at Irchester were in a rather run down condition with most of the plates missing, however, this was not the case with No. 14. This interesting locomotive has survived into preservation, still in the county in which it worked

Another view of No. 14 taken as the locomotive replenishes the water in its tank. This veteran was the oldest locomotive working at Irchester quarry at the time. The other four engines were the Hawthorn Leslies built in the 1930s and two Andrew Barclays built in 1952.

One of the two Andrew Barclays at the Irchester quarries was No. 7, built in 1952 as works no. 2324, seen here filling up at the end of the working day. Note the missing plate from the saddle tank, which probably related to a previous site, the works plate remains however.

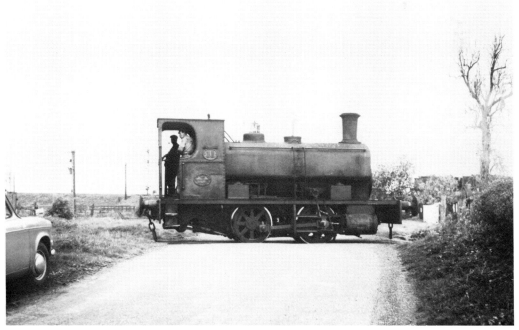

Here No. 11 AB 1047 of 1905 rattles over an ungated crossing on the South Durham Iron & Steel Co. Ltd's Storefield system, on 9 May 1968.

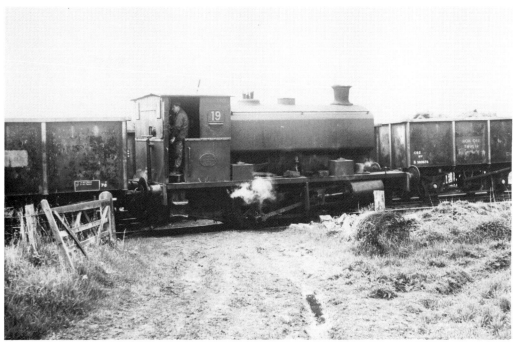

Storefield quarries No. 19 shunts British Railways standard 10-ton iron ore 'tippler' wagons on 9 May 1968. This locomotive is a typical Andrew Barclay design built in 1940 as works no. 2101.

At the Wellingborough ironworks locomotive depot in November 1955 a number of withdrawn veterans were dumped awaiting disposal, among them was No. 6, Hudswell Clarke & Rogers no. 180, of 1876, rebuilt in 1920. This veteran was already eighty years old, and, as can be seen from the photograph, was certainly showing its age.

Another of the locomotives out of use at Wellingborough during the mid-1950s was *The Broke* – a strange name. This 0–4–0ST was built by Andrew Barclay in 1918 as works no. 1592. The locomotive was transferred to Wellingborough from S&L Bilston in 1954.

This sturdy Peckett saddle tank, no. 1235/10 *Forward* had a fine head of steam as it crossed a roadway while shunting ore wagons at Wellingborough ironworks. As with so many industrial sites, there is now nothing to indicate where this large works once stood.

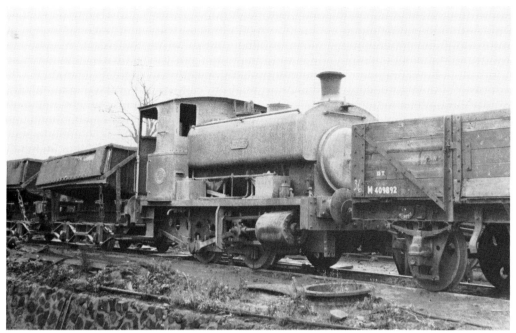

Looking at this photograph of Andrew Barclay 0–4–0ST *Foch*, one is left wondering how long wagons such as the 13-ton example in the foreground were standing around out of general circulation. The locomotive and tipper wagon seen here had obviously not moved for some time. The engine is AB 1645 of 1919 and is pictured at Wellingborough ironworks in November 1955.

Another view of *Forward* as it shunts at Wellingborough, the wagon appears to contain scrap metal for processing. This Peckett had worked at Stanton ironworks, and also Glendon quarries, before being transferred to Wellingborough.

This Hunslet no. 791 of 1902 was originally at Stewart & Lloyds, Corby, moving to Wellingborough ironworks in 1952. Three years later, on 11 November it was lying disused, and the
following month it was scrapped. As can be seen the engine carries the number plate 36, and
nameplate *Isham* from its S&L days.

Wellingboro' No. 5 was on slag disposal duty at Wellingborough ironworks. The locomotive is a
standard 0–4–0ST Andrew Barclay, no. 2063, built in 1939. Locomotives at various sites often
carried names which related to the location involved, as in this case.

The scrap-yard at Wellingborough ironworks was a sad sight in November 1955 with an 0–4–0ST already reduced to pieces, while *Isham*, Hunslet no. 791 of 1902, also awaits its fate. Locomotives at this time were often cut up with nameplates and works plates still in place.

Holwell No. 19 was built by Andrew Barclay of Kilmarnock in 1924 as works no. 1826. As indicated by the locomotive's name, it had worked at the Holwell ironworks of that name before being transferred to Wellingborough.

11.11. 55.

This Andrew Barclay, No. 8, was one of the five locomotives supplied new to Wellingborough ironworks, in this case in 1941, together with a sister engine. The locomotive is seen here working slag-tipping wagons to the tip on a grey November day. The works no. of the locomotive is 2136.

Holwell No. 19 an 0–4–0ST built by Andrew Barclay in 1924 (works no. 1826) carries out shunting duties at Wellingborough ironworks on 11 November 1955. Nothing now remains of the once extensive furnaces and rail systems at this location.

Hawthorn Leslie of Newcastle upon Tyne built this sturdy 0–4–0ST in 1935 (works no. 3813) supplying it new to the Wellingborough ironworks, where it was still at work in 1955.

Wellingboro' Iron Co. Ltd No. 4 was another of the veterans lying out of use at the Wellingborough ironworks in 1955, although it would appear still to be intact at this time. It was a metre gauge locomotive among all the others of standard gauge here. This locomotive was built by Hunslet of Leeds as works no. 473 in 1888, and rebuilt in 1920. The end came when it was cut up in 1959.

Kettering Iron & Coal Co. Ltd., operated a standard gauge rail system at the ironworks, and a 3 ft system in the ironstone quarries. The company became part of the giant S&L group in 1956. This most unusual 0–4–0ST locomotive, shunting at the ironworks on a damp November day in 1955, was a Lingford Gardiner of 1931, which spent many years at Kettering as No. 14. Note the dual sets of buffers fitted.

Oxfordshire Ironstone Company *Newlay* was built by Hunslet of Leeds in 1917 (works no. 1292). Here the locomotive returns empty wagons to the quarry on 24 November 1954.

Alex heads a train of loaded mineral wagons from the Oxfordshire ironstone quarries on a grey November day in 1954. This engine was built by Hunslet in 1952, and it works number is 3716. This ironstone company operated a larger number of locomotives from two depots. The Hunslet in this picture was supplied new to the company.

One could stand in the countryside and watch the activity of the Oxfordshire Ironstone Company locomotives. Here No. 6, *Gwen*, built by Hudswell Clarke (1662/36) drifts by with a train of tipper wagons on 24 November 1954. Considerable activity was to be seen on this line at this time with frequent trains of iron ore, and empties returning from the interchange sidings.

Photographed here in Cohens' Kettering scrap-yard on 3 October 1965 is one of the extensive fleet of locomotives operated by the Oxfordshire Ironstone Company, near Banbury, possibly *Jean*, several of which ended their days at Kettering. At this time Cohens were also involved in cutting up large numbers of British Railways locomotives.

119

This unusual locomotive was built by the Yorkshire Engine Company in 1882 as works no. 327, after changing hands several times it reached Corby steelworks in 1945. It was, incidentally, the only Yorkshire Engine Co. locomotive in the Corby fleet and would certainly have been an interesting subject for preservation.

Stewart & Lloyds No. 27 had certainly seen better days. I was fortunate that a member of staff was able to tow the engine from the depths of the shed where it had resided for a long time, in order to take this photograph. This 'CR Pug' engine was built by the Caledonian Railway at St. Rollox works in 1902, and was then sold as LMS 16037. No. 27 was scrapped six months after this photograph was taken in November 1955.

S&L No. 18 was supplied new to Corby by Hawthorn Leslie in 1936 as works number 3896. Here, in yellow livery, the engine carries out shunting duties on 24 November 1955. A large number of the engines at the steelworks were built by Hawthorn Leslie.

Pen Green was built by Hudswell Clarke in 1903 and supplied new to Corby steelworks. The works no. of this veteran was 607. First impressions of this locomotive indicate a similarity to the Manning Wardle designs.

This smart, powerful 0–6–0ST was built by Robert Stephenson & Hawthorns Ltd in 1941 (works no. 7025) and supplied new to Corby where it became No. 23.

Another view of the veteran Hudswell Clarke 0–6–0ST *Pen Green*. Engines of this type were used by Stewart & Lloyds at many locations. The engine is seen here carrying the S&L No. 3.

Beaumont (S&L No. 28) was built by Hawthorn Leslie in 1900. The engine was busy on shunting duties in the November sunshine in 1955. There was, however, not much time left for No. 28 as it was withdrawn from service in 1958. The locomotive was HL works no. 2469.

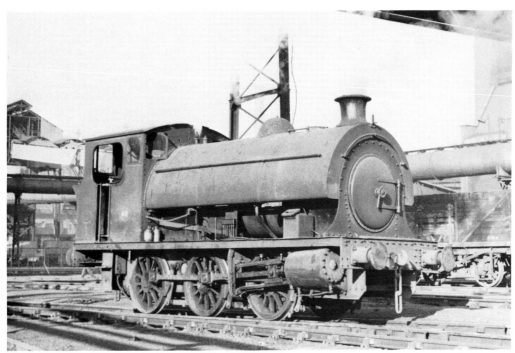

Hawthorn Leslie works no. 3375 was built at Newcastle upon Tyne in 1919, the locomotive is seen here during a brief respite in shunting operations. The fleet No. of HL 3375 was 40.

Stewart & Lloyds No. 9, a sturdy Hudswell Clarke 0–6–0ST, HC 1383/19, had spent its working life in the Corby steelworks. In the mid-1950s a wide variety of steam locomotives built by several companies could be found at work in steelwork yards.

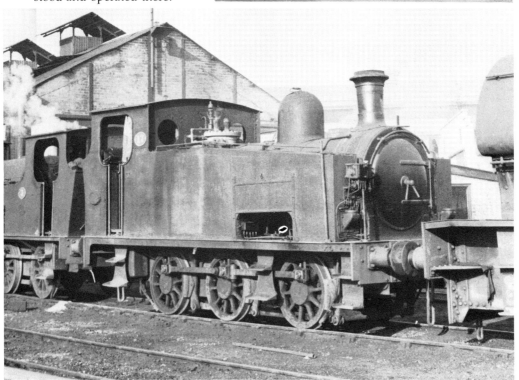

Locomotives built by Pecketts of Bristol were not common at Corby, with just one example in the mid-1950s, the works number of which is 1456, built in 1918. *Margot* came to Corby from the nearby Islip iron-works, near Thrapston in 1950. The site at Islip, which was alongside the Kettering to Huntingdon line, now gives no indication of what once stood and operated there.

All of the locomotives at Corby were various types of saddle tanks with one exception, No. 17, Hudswell Clarke no. 1595 of 1926. One other 0–6–0T design was there until 1936.

Ironworks No. 1, S&L No. 5, was supplied new to Corby in 1911 from its builders Andrew Barclay of Kilmarnock, as works no. 1241. This engine also worked at Wellingborough ironworks for a short time in the early 1950s.

Andrew Barclay 0–6–0ST no. 1457 was built in 1915 and was originally with Shell Mex and BP Ltd, moving to Corby in 1939 where it became No. 29 on the engine list.

Locomotives belonging to Messrs Shanks & McEwan Ltd, a contractor, were also to be found at Corby steelworks. Avonside no. 1435/01 was employed on shunting duties on 12 November 1955. The locomotive carried the nameplate *No. 10 Rosehall*. However, the engine was, by this stage nearing the end of her days as she was scrapped two years later.

Shanks & McEwan also had this veteran Andrew Barclay at Corby steelworks, the engine is works no. 306 of 1888. When photographed the locomotive was standing out of use, and not long after the picture was taken the engine was scrapped.

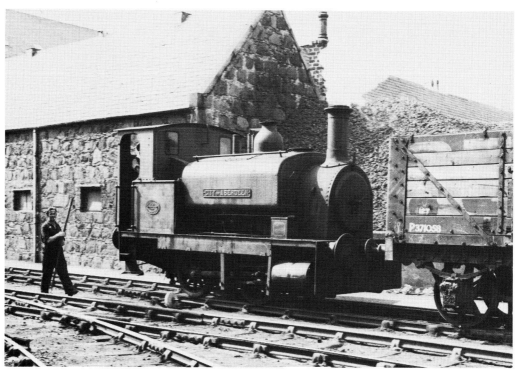

Only four standard gauge locomotives built by Black, Hawthorn & Co. Ltd of Gateshead have survived into preservation. Luckily this veteran, *City of Aberdeen*, built in 1887, owned at one time by the Scottish Gas Board is one of them. Here the engine, works no. 912, is seen shunting at the gasworks sidings in August 1955.

Maud struggles to propel a heavy load of ironstone on the Oxfordshire Ironstone Co. Ltd system, with steam leaking from many parts of the locomotive. *Maud* was built by Pecketts of Bristol in 1938 as works no. 1937, and supplied new to the line.

The fire on this 0–4–0ST, had certainly been dropped for the last time here in this sad scene, as it awaits its fate at Cohens' scrap-yard near Kettering on 3 October 1965. Several of the Oxfordshire ironstone engines were scrapped here at Kettering, a graveyard for a large number of steam engines.

Another view in Cohens' scrap-yard. The engine would appear to be intact, with even valve gear and coupling rods, although the chimney had certainly seen better days, as part of the rim was missing. Note the name- and works plates had gone, unlike the practice in the 1950s when many industrials were cut up with them still in place.

Barabel was one of the post-war Hudswell Clarke 0–4–0STs on the Oxfordshire ironstone system. Here the engine is seen with a train of empties ready to be worked to the quarries. This locomotive, HC 1868 of 1953, was one of the last new engines to be supplied. One other Hudswell Clarke was supplied new in 1953 and a Sentinel in 1956.

24.11.54

Newlay is almost dwarfed by the British Railways wagons it was engaged in shunting. This engine came to the Oxfordshire Ironstone Company from the Margam steel company of Wales in 1951. *Newlay* is Hunslet 0–4–0ST number 1292, built in 1917.

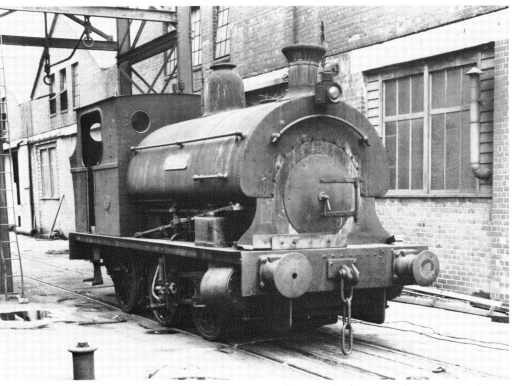

Ronald was under repair in September 1956. This Peckett was built at Bristol in 1907, works no. 1093, being supplied new to the Port of Bristol Authority, Avonmouth docks. Locomotives built by Peckett were very popular at this location, the only other steam locomotives being seven Avonsides, also Bristol-built.

The crew of Peckett no. 1877 of 1934 were surprised when photographs were taken of their engine at the Port of Bristol Authority, Avonmouth docks, in September 1956. *Westbury* is a typical example of the large Peckett saddle tank design.

The last of the nineteen Pecketts to be supplied to the PBA at Avonmouth was this one, Peckett no. 2038 *Redland*, which was delivered in 1943. All the locomotives at Avonmouth were 0–6–0STs, the only exception a P 0–4–0ST, which was sold in 1914.

The sidings at the South Durham Iron & Steel Co. Ltd's Irchester quarry, covered a considerable area as can be seen from this photograph. No. 9 was one of the two sturdy Andrew Barclay 0–4–0STs working at Irchester on 16 March 1967. Its works no. was 2323, and it was built in 1952. The other locomotive was No. 7, AB 2324, also built in 1952.

Judging by the size of the hosepipe, the tank of Hawthorn Leslie no. 3946 of 1937 would take a considerable time to fill up, although this no doubt provided a welcomed break for the crew. This locomotive was No. 17, photographed at the South Durham Iron & Steel Co. Ltd's Irchester quarries on 17 March 1966.

Rhondda S&L Minerals Ltd No. 42, was stored at Harlaxton quarries when this photograph was taken in June 1966. This engine, although very similar in appearance to the Kitsons used by S&L is in fact a Manning Wardle, works no. 2010, built at Leeds in 1921.

Holwell No. 30 was to be found at Irchester quarries in December 1965. This Hawthorn Leslie was built in 1932 as works no. 3780. At this time two Hawthorn Leslies were at work on the line, together with two Andrew Barclays and a Manning Wardle.

This neat 0–4–0ST was built by W.G. Bagnall of Stafford in 1907, and was still going strong on the Storefield quarry system in November 1965. The works no. of *Enterprise* is 1739. The South Durham Iron & Steel Co. Ltd's Storefield site operated five locomotives, the Bagnall, a Peckett and three Andrew Barclays; normally four were in steam daily.

Locomotives were frequently moved from site to site during the last years of operations on the quarry systems. No. 6, Andrew Barclay no. 1496 of 1916, had recently moved to Irchester quarries when this photograph was taken in August 1967. This locomotive was at one time at nearby Storefield quarries.

An indication of the track conditions on some quarry systems can be seen in the background of this photograph. Andrew Barclay No. 20, works no. 2143 of 1942, heads three loaded iron ore wagons through the Northamptonshire countryside on the Storefield system during April 1967.

Glenden quarries near Kettering were part of the large Stewart & Lloyds Ltd operations. In March 1967 three locomotives were at this location, two were normally used daily. Two were Kitsons as seen here, in this case No. 49 *Caerphilly*, works no. 5477 built in 1936. The other engine, built by this company was K5478/36 *Carmarthen*, the third was a Hunslet 0–6–0ST.

Very few locomotives owned by the Southern Railway passed into private ownership. This B4 class 0–4–0T was owned by Corralls Ltd of Southampton. The engine is seen here in March 1967, carrying its new name *Corrall Queen*, also its BR front numberplate and Eastleigh shedplate (71A).

Another view of B4 30096 *Corrall Queen* when owned by Corralls Ltd, set against a backdrop of dock cranes etc. This locomotive was built by the LSWR in 1893 and carried the name *Normandy*. Fortunately, it still survives on the Bluebell Railway; only one other of the twenty-five strong class survives.

Bonnie Prince Charlie is seen here out of use at Corralls Ltd, Southampton, in March 1967. This locomotive was built by Robert Stephenson & Hawthorn in 1949 as works no. 7544. As with the B4 from this location (Ex 30096) *Bonnie Prince Charlie* is now in preservation.

Industrials in Preservation

We are fortunate that a large number of industrial locomotives have been preserved, including many unique engines, such as the 0–4–4–0 Beyer Garratt, *William Francis*, which was owned by the National Coal Board and worked at Baddesley Colliery. Unfortunately, this locomotive is not in working order at present time, being on static display at Bressingham Steam Museum, Norfolk.

One veteran that is very active is the 1874 0–6–0WT *Bellerophon*, now preserved on the Keighley and Worth Valley Railway. This interesting locomotive is occasionally loaned to other railway systems, and is often to be seen working on the KWVR.

Many of the preserved railways operating today, would find it very difficult without engines which came from industrial systems. The Ffestiniog Railway would very much miss the Penrhyn Quarry's, *Linda* and *Blanche*, now rebuilt as 2–4–0STs, which have worked a great many trains over the Ffestiniog in the last few years.

The narrow gauge locomotives were much sought after when offered for sale. Who would have thought these small tank locomotives, which spent their working lives on the bleak exposed galleries of a Welsh slate quarry, would provide the motive power for railway systems in Norfolk, Hampshire and elsewhere, some very close to where they worked for all those years, while others were even to cross the North Atlantic for preservation.

Unfortunately, it is also a sad fact that many other industrials stand in a condition similar to that in which they were purchased. Many have received little, if any, attention, while others will almost certainly never steam again, due to their condition and the large sums of money involved in restoration. Not many years ago technical problems would have prevented any restoration of some locomotives. Now with the aid of modern technology these problems no longer exist, the overriding problem remaining is that of the cost involved.

However, a great many industrials *are* to be seen carefully and painstakingly restored, working in first-class mechanical condition – a fitting tribute to the British companies and engineers that built them, in some cases, a great many years ago.

For many years the ex-Penrhyn slate quarry 0–4–0ST, *George Sholto*, has worked trains on the 'Nursery Railway' at Bressingham Steam Museum. This engine is an example of the Penrhyn 'Large Quarry' class built at Hunslets in 1909 as works no. 994.

Dolbadarn photographed at the Llanberis Lake Railway in September 1971, not far from the Dinorwic slate quarries. This Hunslet was built in 1922, works no. 1430, and is an example of the Dinorwic 'Port' class. The three members of this class were built with cabs. On p.22 the engine is shown working on the Dinorwic without a cab which has only been reinstated in preservation.

Lilla was once in the derelict engine row on the Penrhyn. Here the engine is seen working at Knebworth Park in July 1983. *Lilla* was a non-standard Penrhyn locomotive built by Hunslets in 1891 as works no. 554. The engine is at the present time at the Kew Bridge Museum.

141

For a period of time this Andrew Barclay narrow gauge locomotive *The Doll* was at Bressingham, where it was photographed in August 1966. Barclays built this 0–6–0T in 1919 as works no. 1641. For many years this engine was owned by S&L of Bilston and subsequently Sydenham Ironstone. *The Doll* is now on the Leighton Buzzard Railway.

Only the frames and wheels of *Bronllwyd* were in the Penrhyn scrap road, see p. 28, the boiler and cab having been used to rebuild another locomotive. This Hudswell Clarke works no. 1643 of 1930 has been rebuilt, and is seen in service at Bressingham.

Another very unusual industrial locomotive is the 0–4–4–0T built by W.G. Bagnall Ltd of Stafford for the 2 ft 6 in gauge system of the Bowaters Paper Mills at Sittingbourne, Kent. *Monarch* seems a very appropriate name for this stately locomotive. Its works no. is 3024 and it was built in 1953. For many years this locomotive has been at the Welshpool & Llanfair Railway where this photograph was taken.

The ex-Penrhyn Hunslet *Linda* stands at Portmadoc ready to work another train. The engine is seen here still running as an 0–4–0ST. Since photographed this fine Hunslet has been converted to a 2–4–0.

The two Penrhyn slate quarry locomotives which became part of the Ffestiniog Railway locomotive fleet, have been, and still are invaluable. Here a shining *Linda*, Hunslet 590 of 1893, stands ready to leave Portmadoc not long after joining the Ffestiniog. Both of the Hunslets are now rebuilt to 2–4–0 wheel arrangement.

The Hunslet 0–4–0ST *Maid Marion* was at Bressingham for a short time, it is seen here raising steam in September 1968. *Maid Marion* was a Dinorwic engine, HE 822 of 1903, and is at present time on the Bala Light Railway.

Eigiau, Orenstein & Koppel 0–4–0WT no. 5668 of 1912, looking very different to the condition in which it was photographed in the early 1960s, see p.27. This picture shows the engine in service on the 'Nursery Line' at Bressingham Steam Museum, a far cry indeed from an isolated slate gallery on the Penrhyn slate quarry system.

Another of the Dinorwic slate quarry engines, this time No. 1, Hunslet no. 1429 of 1922, at Woburn Abbey in August 1968. This engine is another of the Dinorwic 'Port' class which were all built with cabs, most of the locomotives on the system not having such a luxury.

Metre gauge Corpet 0–6–0T no. 493 *Cambrai* was built in 1888. For a number of years it was at the Tywyn Narrow Gauge Museum. This locomotive worked at the Loddington ironstone quarries, arriving there from Chemin de Fer du Cambresis, France in 1936.

This veteran Hunslet 0–4–0ST spent its working life on the Penrhyn slate quarries. *Gwynedd* is works no. 316 built in 1883. This fine narrow gauge engine is one of the mainstays at the Bressingham Steam Museum, where it has been since purchased from North Wales.

Over the years many different locomotives have been at the Bressingham Steam Museum, some moving on to other locations in time, as did this metre gauge Peckett 0–6–0ST once owned by S&L Minerals Ltd at Wellingborough, where, in company with the line's other two Pecketts, it was a common sight crossing the Wellingborough to Finedon road.

This most unusual industrial locomotive is Beyer Peacock 0–4–0 + 0–4–0 works no. 6841, built in 1937. *William Francis* spent its working life with the National Coal Board at Baddesley Colliery, Warwickshire. This locomotive is part of the static display at Bressingham Steam Museum.

This veteran 0–4–0 saddle tank was built by Sharp Stewart for the Furness Railway as an 0–4–0 tender locomotive, No. 25, in 1865 as works no. 1585. It was withdrawn by the FR in 1873 and sold, eventually becoming Barrow steelworks No. 17. This locomotive and FR 18, built in 1863, are at Steamtown, Carnforth, where this photograph was taken in May 1986.

Hudswell Clarke 1539 of 1924, *Derek Crouch*, was exhibited at the 1973 Expo Steam event held at the Alwalton showground near Peterborough – note the fairground rides in the background. This 0–6–0ST is preserved by the Nene Valley Railway. Its last working location was the NCB opencast site at Widdrington, Northumberland.

The famous Haydock Foundry 0–6–0WT was built in 1874. This very interesting locomotive has been superbly restored and is regularly in steam. *Bellerophon* was owned by the National Coal Board at Lea Green Colliery, Lancashire, and is now to be found on the Keighley and Worth Valley Railway.

The Lady Armaghdale, Hunslet 0–6–0T no. 686 of 1898, has proved a very useful addition to the fleet of locomotives on the Severn Valley Railway. During its working life it was owned by ICI Dyestuffs of Blackley Works, Manchester.

This very interesting 0–4–0 crane tank was built by Andrew Barclay of Kilmarnock in 1902 as works no. 880, *Glenfield*, and was owned by Messrs Glenfield & Kennedy also of Kilmarnock. During preservation this locomotive has been at several railway centres, photographed in July 1977 at Tyseley.

Sentinel no. 7232 was built in 1927. This photograph was taken on the Yorkshire Dales Railway in April 1973 when the locomotive stood in the yard. As can partly be seen, the engine's owners were British Tar Products Ltd of Irham, Lancashire.

Avonside 0–4–0ST works no. 1908 was built in 1925 and was owned by ICI of Tunstead. In this 1973 photograph the locomotive is seen working a passenger train on the Yorkshire Dales Railway at Embsay. This locomotive moved on to an owner in Belgium.

Hunslets of this type were very popular with the National Coal Board and other companies. *Beatrice* is HE no. 2705 of 1949, seen here at the Yorkshire Dales Railway in 1990.

Primrose No. 2 prepares to leave Embsay station on the Yorkshire Dales Railway with a passenger train. This engine was built by Hunslet in 1951, as works no. 3715, ending its working days at NCB Peckfield Colliery.

The Hunslet *Jacks Green* seen here in operation on the Nene Valley Railway not long after being purchased from the nearby Nassington & Barrowden Mining Co. *Jacks Green* is HE no. 1953 of 1939, the other similar locomotive from Nassington, *Ring Haw* is on the North Norfolk Railway at Sheringham.

Jane Darbyshire is Andrew Barclay no. 1969 of 1929, which was owned by British Gypsum of Cocklakes Works, Cumwhinton, Cumbria. This 1972 photograph was taken at Steamtown, Carnforth, and shows the engine in superb condition.

Neilson & Co. built this locomotive with cut-down mountings in 1896 as works no. 5087. It was supplied new to the North Thames Gas Board, Beckton gasworks, and carried No. 25. During its working lifetime it was rebuilt on site in 1938. Here the engine is in steam, shortly after entering preservation at Bressingham Steam Museum, Norfolk.

Several of the 0–4–0 crane tanks of William Doxford & Sons Ltd's Pallion Shipyard, Sunderland, have fortunately been preserved. Here one of those preserved stands at Bressingham, Norfolk, its new home, in October 1971 shortly after delivery. *Millfield*, works no. 7070 of 1942, was built by Robert Stephenson & Hawthorns Ltd, and supplied new to the shipyard.

Another photograph of No. 25 showing how the Britannia 70013 *Oliver Cromwell* towers over the Neilson saddle tank. This unique Neilson engine has been a static exhibit for some considerable time.

Pitsford photographed on the Nene Valley Railway shortly after being rescued for preservation. The Avonside 0–6–0ST was built in 1923 as works no. 1917, working for the Byfield Ironstone Co., Byfield, Northants. As with many other industrials this engine has now moved on, being at present time at Steamtown, Carnforth.

Several locomotives were fitted with ungainly gas producer chimneys during their last years in service, such as NCB S.134, *Wheldale*, seen here in preservation on the Yorkshire Dales Railway.